What people ar
Sekhı

Sekhmet is a Goddess for today's world. She fiercely protects right order, returning balance to the world, and just as fiercely protects those who celebrate Her. Her name means "Powerful Woman" and She symbolizes courage and strength as well as inspiration and comfort. This book examines the ancient Egyptian devotion to Sekhmet, utilizing Egyptian sources and analyzing their puzzling complexity in such a way as to make them accessible to the modern reader. Sekhmet's qualities as a healer are explored, as well as Her role within the Egyptian pantheon, the temples and cults dedicated to Her, and the rituals, festivals, magic, and prayers that centered on Her. At the same time, it explores the way in which Sekhmet is increasingly cherished and worshipped today, offering suggestions for practice and ways to adapt her ancient rituals to today's world. This book is a must read for Sekhmet devotees and for those who are looking for a Goddess for these times.

Candace C. Kant, Ph.D. Academic Dean Cherry Hill Seminary, co-editor of *Heart of the Sun: An Anthology in Exaltation of Sekhmet.*

This is a very comprehensive book on the ancient Egyptian Goddess Sekhmet. Myths, rituals and magic all included and more. Church has blended together a good mix of history and modern perspectives. A fascinating book.

Rachel Patterson, author of the *Kitchen Witchcraft* series, *The Cailleach* and *The Triple Goddess*

Pagan Portals - Sekhmet is an excellent well researched and substantial guide to this powerful and well-loved Egyptian goddess, written with clarity and passion by someone who is equally academically sound and spiritually inspired. Olivia Church guides us through the primary sources and archaeological evidence of the worship of Sekhmet as well as making use of modern scholarship to produce a book that is both spiritually rich in insight and sensibly grounded in up to date research. A real treasure and especially relevant to our times. Highly recommended.

Danu Forest, MA. Priestess of Isis, Celtic Scholar and traditional wisewoman. Author of *Gwyn ap Nudd, wild God of faerie* and *Celtic Tree Magic- ogham lore and druid mysteries*

I have long been intrigued by the Egyptian Goddess Sekhmet and was therefore very much looking to reading Olivia Church's book on this subject. This book did not disappoint! Church unravels the complexities that exist in Sekhmet's myths and titles, therefore making this Goddess even more approachable for both devotees and those who may have been interested in Sekhmet but have been intimidated by her as well. 'Sekhmet' shines a light on aspects of the Goddess that are not always fully understood, such as her roles in healing and protection. Church's book is well researched and timely, and I would highly recommend it to anyone who has an interest in exploring Egyptian myth and deities.

Robin Corak, author of *Pagan Portals – Persephone: Practicing the Art of Personal Power.*

Pagan Portals
Sekhmet

Eye of Ra, Lady of Flame

Pagan Portals
Sekhmet

Eye of Ra, Lady of Flame

Olivia Church

**MOON
BOOKS**
Winchester, UK
Washington, USA

JOHN HUNT PUBLISHING

First published by Moon Books, 2021
Moon Books is an imprint of John Hunt Publishing Ltd., No. 3 East Street, Alresford
Hampshire SO24 9EE, UK
office@jhpbooks.net
www.johnhuntpublishing.com
www.moon-books.net

For distributor details and how to order please visit the 'Ordering' section on our website.

Text copyright: Olivia Church 2021

ISBN: 978 1 78904 713 4
978 1 78904 714 1 (ebook)
Library of Congress Control Number: 2020950148

A CIP catalogue record for this book is available from the British Library.

Design: Matthew Greenfield

UK: Printed and bound by CPI Group (UK) Ltd, Croydon, CR0 4YY
Printed in North America by CPI GPS partners

We operate a distinctive and ethical publishing philosophy in
all areas of our business, from our global network of authors to
production and worldwide distribution.

Contents

*This book is dedicated to all those who, in justified anger,
stand up in defence of our planet, its people, and all creatures.*

Acknowledgements

This book was born from the trail blazed by its predecessor, *Isis: Great of Magic, She of 10,000 Names*. Hopping across the hot embers of this work, I was moved to embark on a journey exploring the contradictory nature of the ancient Egyptian Goddess, Sekhmet. Facing this lioness divinity head-first is no easy task. It was clear to me that different people today seek Sekhmet for various reasons: some approach her as the embodiment of Divine Feminine power and as a protective Goddess, who watches over her cubs and inspires rage at the injustices of the modern world; others beseech her for healing and help in dire situations; and others approach her as the burning Eye of Ra, the cause and first responder to disease and otherworldly dangers. Though some question her contemporary relevance as a violent war-Goddess, other devotees revel in her uncompromising aggression. These dynamic interpretations inspired me to delve deeper, to ask how the ancients may have understood her, and to explore why her worship today is ever growing!

As a contribution to the Pagan Portals series, I wish for this book to be accessible to Pagan readers who are both curious about and inspired by Sekhmet. I believe that everyone should have access to up-to-date historical knowledge, in addition to valuing modern innovations and personal gnosis; therefore, I include both approaches in this work, endeavouring to distinguish between the two.

This is a devotional journey to Sekhmet, who I thank for her ability to fill me with determination and the courage to consume my (metaphorical and not so metaphorical) adversaries and challenges. I wish to extend a special thanks to my teacher and friend, Caroline Wise, who has always encouraged me to stand in my own power. I also want to thank everyone who has been so supportive during the release of 'Isis', especially my partner, who would not stop mentioning how proud of me they were! As with my previous book, my dear friend Ronnie has been a great help for writing 'Sekhmet', lending me her wisdom and impressive knowledge. I am grateful to Candace Kant, a long-standing Priestess of Sekhmet, who helped me explore Sekhmet's diverse nature, beyond the Egyptological textbooks. I also thank Pam Evans, friend and founder of the Peace Mala charity, for helping me learn more about *Seichim* healing and polish off this book! Finally, I want to express my gratitude to Trevor Greenfield, who has been ever patient and supportive of me and my work for the series so far.

Senebty
May you be healthy!

Abbreviations

CT – Coffin Texts
PT – Pyramid Texts
BRP – Bremner-Rhind Papyrus

Timeline
(Dates provided from Shaw, 2003)

Early Dynasty Period
Comprising Dynasties 1 & 2, 3000-2686 BCE

Old Kingdom
Comprising Dynasties 3-8, 2686-2160 BCE

First Intermediate Period
Comprising Dynasties 9 & 10, 2160-2055 BCE

Middle Kingdom
Comprising Dynasties 11-14, 2055-1650 BCE

Second Intermediate Period
Comprising Dynasties 15-17, 1650-1550 BCE

New Kingdom (Including Ramesside Period)
Comprising Dynasties 18-20, 1550-1069 BCE

Third Intermediate Period
Comprising Dynasties 21-25, 1069-664 BCE

Late Period
Comprising Dynasties 26-30 & 2nd Persian Period, 664-332 BCE

Graeco-Roman Period
Comprising Macedonian & Ptolemaic Dynasties, 332-30 BCE
Roman Period, 30 BCE – 395 CE

Map of Featured Ancient Egyptian Sites

Introduction

Sekhmet (also written Sakhmet) is instantly recognisable today from her fierce appearance, bearing the proud head of a lioness, crowned by the sun disc and cobra, with the lower body of an Egyptian woman. As with many Egyptian deities, Sekhmet is a complex character with a dramatic mythology and enduring influence, which continues to inspire people today. Her name, *sḫm.t* translates to 'The Powerful (female) One' and serves as an effective proclamation of her ancient might. Sekhmet is often seen in connection to the cat Goddess, Bastet, and the bovine Goddess Hut-hor (pronounced *Hoot-hor*, Greek Hathor); though sufficiently distinct, these Goddesses are often syncretised, making it oftentimes unavoidable to explore one without the other. Nevertheless, though Bastet and Hut-hor often feature upon the pages of this book, it will nonetheless remain emphatically about Sekhmet.

Sekhmet is a challenging Goddess and this introductory volume will present her without airs and graces. She was the patron of healers and doctor-priests with an unrivalled ability to both inflict and retract illness and disease, bringing great harm as well as offering healing and fierce protection (Wilkinson, 2003, p. 182). It was not just thankfulness for these gifts that made her cult popular, for Sekhmet inspired great fear and needed to be appeased to ensure her blessing. She was a blood-thirsty warrior Goddess who brought death, fear, and suffering. Sekhmet therefore represents ancient human fears which continue to affect people across the globe today. It is Sekhmet's wild, terrifying, and untamed nature that many find so intriguing. She is a Goddess of contradiction, sovereign over violence and sickness, as well as patron of healing and protection; she truly is the Mighty One.

Today Sekhmet often bears the title 'Goddess of Healing',

relegating her to this specific realm of influence. The practice of categorising Pagan deities in this way has its origins in antiquarianism, seeking to minimise the scope of power for polytheistic deities (in comparison to the all-encompassing power of a monotheistic god). Though often helpful for introducing Pagans to these deities today, such minimisation is anachronistic and does not reflect ancient Egyptian concepts of deity. Ancient Egyptian deities (as with many other ancient pantheons) were extremely complex, with powers intersecting with numerous aspects of life and death. Identifying Sekhmet as 'Goddess of Healing' implies that this was her primary area of concern and divine occupation. It is true that many of her priests were also doctors and that people often prayed to her for healing; however, numerous ancient texts also describe her as the cause for disease in the first place. Many modern Pagans prefer to emphasise her healing attributes, which is completely valid. But it is vital that we recognise her dangerous aspects also, as the unleashed manifestation of female rage and nature's destructive forces. At times nature can be harrowing. This is a fact of life, reflected in many of Goddesses and Gods across world cultures.

Before we begin it is important to introduce you to the ancient Egyptian words for deities that I shall be using from now on. I choose to use these ancient Egyptian words, as well as the Egyptian versions of deities' names in order to remain true to their origins. Ancient Egyptian male Gods were known as *nṯr,* plural *nṯr.w* (roughly pronounced *necher* and *necheru*). The female Goddesses were known as *nṯr.t,* plural *nṯr.wt* (which can be pronounced *necheret* and *necheroot*). Throughout this text I will capitalise these words as proper nouns and transcribe them into an anglicised rendering for ease of reading, thus: Netjer, Netjeru, Netjeret, Netjerut.

The following chapters of this book will delve into Sekhmet's mythology, excavating her destructive and healing aspects. Her role as the Eye of Ra and subsequent connection to other Egyptian Netjerut will be discussed, as well as the ways in which she was worshipped by the ancient Egyptians, in daily life, in temples, and at festivals. Each chapter will end with the provision of a contemporary Pagan perspective, bringing Sekhmet's ancient origins into modern relevance. This book will conclude with an overview of her worship today, which is ever expanding! Before we begin this journey, I will now introduce Sekhmet in her ancient Egyptian context.

A North African Deity

I wish to emphasise Sekhmet's context as a North African deity whose origins and ancient worship were firmly located within the Egyptian landscape and cultural worldview. This is important to remember, not only because the land itself explains much about her character, but also because there are many contemporary Pagans today who are not of North African descent and who live outside of Egypt, reviving her worship abroad. Sekhmet did not receive the same enthusiastic reception from the Graeco-Roman world that Netjerut such as Aset (Greek Isis) did. Whatever the reason for this, Sekhmet has maintained a distinctly Egyptian and Nubian identity. Wherever possible, I advocate that one keeps this context in mind, paying due respect to the beliefs of the ancient Egyptian ancestors, as well as towards the living descendants who reside in these landscapes today, and whose heritage we offer the greatest respect to.

Sekhmet's character and mythology were formed from the flowing waters, the desert sands, and intense sun of Egypt's ancient landscape. One of the names that the ancient Egyptians knew their land by was *km.t* or *kemet,* meaning the 'black land', after the black soil of the Nile banks (Brewer & Teeter, 2007, p. 22). *Kemet* was, and Egypt is, a valley of fecund fields, swaying palms, and ripe fruits. Sailing along the river is a feast of colour, from its piercing blue sky, to its lush green foliage, and gleaming

3

yellow mountains in the distance. The river is cradled between the eastern and western mountains, reminding you that the desert resides close by. For ancient and modern Egyptians, the intensity of the Egyptian summer sun was, and is, a very real fact of life. In ancient times the end of the summer consisted of scorching heat and parched fields and people eagerly awaited the coming of the flood, which occurred annually until the establishment of the Aswan High Dam in 1970. Contrastingly, the winter months welcomed cooler temperatures with inundated fields, rich soil, and abundant crop growth (Brewer & Teeter, 2007, pp. 21, 31).

This dichotomy formed an Egyptian worldview of the balance between order and chaos, physically expressed through the luscious floodplain and the arid desert. The river valley where the Egyptian people settled and built their civilisation was considered the realm of order, under the jurisdiction of the Pharaoh, the embodiment of the Netjer Heru on earth (Greek Horus). The desert on the other hand was an unoccupied, mysterious landscape, exposed to the creatures of chaos and the sovereignty of the Netjer Sutekh (Greek Seth; Wilkinson, 2003, p. 197).

Though certainly worshipped in the floodplain settlements, Sekhmet could be found roaming the outskirts and places suited to the habitat of lions and land predators. Sekhmet was very much a Netjeret tied to the landscape from which she originated, reflected by her associations with sunlight, heat, fire, and the untamed wild. It is easy to understand Sekhmet's destructive qualities when one considers the intensity of the Egyptian sun that she embodies. Whilst other Egyptian Netjeru represent beneficent solar qualities, Sekhmet embodies its destructive potential, that which burns, consumes, and causes drought. Her fiery breath can be felt on especially hot days, where heat waves are visible before your very eyes (Wilkinson, 2003, p. 181). On days such as this, one can tangibly feel the lioness's hot breath panting over them, burning skin, causing thirst...

4

An Egyptian Lioness

Wild animals roamed the desert and the Nile valley alike, although with time larger predators were over-hunted or chose to move down river. There are several leonine deities within the ancient Egyptian pantheon, with a clear predominance of female lionesses. Sekhmet is iconic amongst them and her manifestation as a lioness is integral to her nature.

Leonine imagery is attested during the Predynastic period of Egypt, around 3200-3000 BCE, found carved on ceremonial palettes. According to common (though also contested) theory, schematic versions of these palettes originally functioned as plates for the grinding and subsequent application of cosmetics, which were potentially worn during hunting rituals (Wilkinson, 2003, p. 94). More elaborate ceremonial palettes began to appear during the Naqada III period, suggesting an elite interest in hunting; this is supported by zooarchaeological evidence, indicating that meat consumption occupied a minimal percentage of common diets despite considerable iconographic representation (Hendrickx et al, 2010, 17, 19-20; Hendrickx, 2013, p. 238). The ritual hunt was a symbolic display of order triumphing over chaos, expressed by human hunters defeating wild prey. On the *Hunter's Palette* lions are amongst the animals chosen to embody the chaotic wild to be conquered (British Museum, EA20792; Wilkinson, 2003, p.100). Elsewhere, the lion embodied the power of the ruler himself, mutilating human enemies on the *Battlefield Palette* (British Museum, EA20791). Perhaps this was due to a recognition of the social organisation, strength, and hunting prowess of lions. Such a dramatic image is one to remember when exploring Sekhmet's mythology in the chapter that follows.

Figure 1. The Battlefield Palette (British Museum, EA20791)

During this early period several kinds of lions lived in the Nile Valley. Though they gradually left at the dawn of Egypt's historical period, lions continued to feature as an important religious and royal symbol (Pinch, 2002, p. 133). There is a good reason that it was deemed impressive to hunt and kill one, or to impersonate their power in iconography.

Sekhmet's alignment with the lioness meant that she was believed to possess a ferocious protectiveness over her cubs and undertook the responsibility of leading the pride's merciless hunt for food. Both these roles - ensuring protection and obtaining food – necessitates a violence in the animal kingdom which is

6

required to maintain nature's balance. As this book will not shy away from Sekhmet's violent nature and blood-stained maw, it is essential to understand this in the context of the lioness, rather than strictly envisioning human violence – which is too often committed for reasons other than survival.

Earliest Historical Appearance

The earliest attestation of Sekhmet's name dates to Egypt's Old Kingdom in the *Pyramid Texts* (abbreviated hereafter, *PT*), around 2631-2181 BCE. These texts are inscriptions found within the earliest pyramids in Egypt, predating those located on the famous Giza complex. To some, these pyramids might not look like much from the outside, but inside the walls are covered in columns upon columns of magical hieroglyphic texts. These consist of sacred utterances intended to ensure the Pharaoh's ascension into the afterlife by magic and divine assistance. It is here that Sekhmet is first mentioned by name and in connection to two other feline Netjerut, Bastet and Shezmetet (Lange, 2016, p. 304). In one utterance Sekhmet and Shezmetet are joint mothers of the Pharaoh:

I [the Pharaoh] *have emerged from the Ennead's thighs.*
I have been conceived by Sekhmet, and Shezmetet is the one who gave birth to me...
(*PT Unis,* 248; trans. Allen, James P. 2015)

Such a statement demonstrates the ability for ancient Egyptian religion to hold multiple seemingly contradictory truths at once. The *PT* appear very early on in ancient Egyptian history with no clear antecedents; however, they are so well developed that scholars have surmised that their mythic context must predate their recording within the pyramids (Malek, 2003, p. 102). Therefore, though Sekhmet's name appears here for the very first time in writing, it is likely that she had a religious presence much earlier than this. By the 5th dynasty the cult of Sekhmet is well attested, as a particular favourite of the Pharaoh Sahure (Gaber, 2003, p. 18). The *PT* references to Sekhmet and her close connection to Sahure, tell us that from the beginning of Egyptian history she could be regarded as the mother of Pharaohs. These rulers inherited the throne of Egypt through their maternal link with Netjerut such as Sekhmet, the daughter of Ra, the Creator Himself.

Now it is time to explore Sekhmet's mythology, uncovering the stories that the Egyptians used to understand her behaviour and interaction with the human world.

Chapter 1

Mythology

Creation & The 'Becoming' of Sekhmet

There exist multiple versions of the creation myth known to the ancient Egyptians, depending on geographic region, cult centre, and time. The Heliopolitan creation myth is one that is most relevant to Sekhmet and was once popular in the area around modern-day Cairo. Most deities within the Heliopolitan pantheon have a traditional mother-father parentage, aside from the Creator himself and his first twin offspring. Sekhmet's origins are less a story of birth and more a story of *becoming*; we therefore need to begin with the origins of her sister, Tefnut.

Consistent with many other creation myths, in the beginning there was nothing, and then there was something... To the Egyptians, this 'nothing' was a dark watery expanse known as the *Nun*. For a reason beyond the comprehension of humankind, the Creator Netjer emerged from this space and chose to do what Creators do best, and create (Pinch, 2002, pp. 58-59). According to the Heliopolitan creation myth, this Creator was Atum-Ra who was 'the father and mother of all things.' The Egyptian word for 'hand' was the feminine noun *dr.t* or *deret,* which could be personified by the sensual Netjeret Hut-hor (Pinch, 2002, p. 136). This is significant, for it explained how the male Creator was able to create life from his union with his Hand; indeed, *PT* 527 records how in an act of self-pleasure Atum-Ra produced the primordial twins, Shu and Tefnut. An alternative explanation occurs later in the *PT*, claiming that the pair were born from within the Creator's mouth and were subsequently spat out (*PT* 600; Pinch, 2002, p. 63). Whatever the method, the first divine siblings were born from the Creator's body as 'the one who developed into three'. Thus, Atum-Ra brought the primordial elements of air and moisture into being.

Shu and Tefnut could be depicted as a pair of twin lions, who sat back to back looking out towards each horizon with the sun Netjer safe between them. In this form, each one looked out upon the rising and setting sun and represented the concept of time, of yesterday and tomorrow (Pinch, 2002, p. 197). The combination of air and moisture, under the heat of the sun led to the birth of the next generation of deities: the earth Netjer Geb and sky Netjeret Nut (pronounced *Noot*). As the Netjer of air and the breath of life, Shu took his place separating the earth and the sky so that life could grow in the space between them (Pinch, 2002, p. 65). From their union sprung Wesir, Sutekh, Aset, and Nebet-hut (Greek Osiris, Seth, Isis, and Nephthys), completing the group of deities known as the Heliopolitan Ennead. Heru is sometimes included within this group, either as a sibling, or as a child of Wesir and Aset. Finally, Tefnut took her place as the protective Eye of her father, as the embodiment of the sun, shining light upon creation so that the Creator could see all things. Whilst the Eye is always the daughter of the solar Creator, one may find that his name varies, from Atum, Ra, Khepri, Ptah, and many other syncretised forms (Pinch, 2002, p. 153); however, the Eye herself was referred to as the Eye of Ra (sometimes the Eye of Heru), to emphasise her solar role. For consistencies sake, I will now refer to the Creator in the following myths as Ra.

There exist two primary myths relating to the Daughter / Eye of Ra, which both follow a similar structure. For this reason, it may be easy to get the two confused; however, they should be viewed as two distinct stories. In my reading it makes most sense to view the Myth of the Wandering / Distant Goddess as taking place first, although others, such as Nicki Scully read them the opposite way around (Scully, 2017, pp. 17-18).

The Myth of the Eye of the Sun
(The Wandering / Distant Goddess)

Egyptian mythology is rarely recorded in a linear narrative and is instead found across several sources. For this reason, there are many versions that exist with slight variations which may cause readers uncertainty, though all versions can be considered equally 'correct'. The Myth of the Eye of the Sun is also known as the Myth of the Wandering / Distant Goddess and is recorded upon the walls of over twenty Ptolemaic temples (Richter, 2010, p. 156). The Ptolemaic period can be dated to between 332-30 BCE. Though this is a relatively late period of Egyptian history, snippets of the myth can also be found much earlier. Conveniently for us, this fragmented myth was pieced together in the early 20th century by Hermann Junker, providing us with a coherent narrative (Junker, 1911). According to this compilation, the myth took place during a time when the Creator still lived upon the earth as ruler of Egypt, with his Eye, Tefnut by his side. One day, for unspecified reasons, Tefnut decided to leave her father and wandered south to Nubia (modern day Sudan).

Ra missed his daughter's company almost as much as he feared the loss of protection conferred by her fiery gaze. In some versions the risk of being without her protection was too great, leading Ra to create a replacement Eye in Tefnut's absence (Pinch, 2002, p. 64). A spell from the earlier Middle Kingdom *Coffin Texts* (hereafter *CT*), records that her brother, Shu, had left with her, provoking their father to come looking for them:

Atum once sent his Sole Eye seeking me and my sister, Tefnut.
(*CT* 76, translated by Faulkner, 2007)

Perhaps it was Tefnut's indignance that convinced her to return, for upon her arrival she expressed her fury at being replaced. Some sources state that humanity was born from her tears, making a play on words between the word for tear, *remyt*, and the word for people, *remech*. (Pinch, 2002, pp. 66, 129; Faulkner, 1962, p. 149) This distress was not long-lasting, however, as seeking to quickly appease her, Ra placed Tefnut proudly upon his forehead as the first uraeus serpent (Pinch, 2002, p. 64). Tefnut's return was celebrated with festivities, where she bathed in the sacred waters of Philae and transformed from a lioness into a beautiful woman. According to Barbara Richter, these temple texts acted as an outline for a real festival which took place in celebration of the Netjeret's mythic return (explored further in Chapter 6; Richter, 2010). Although Sekhmet has not yet been mentioned by name, each of the Eyes of Ra could be interpreted as aspects of one another. Not only are Tefnut and Sekhmet both lioness daughters of Ra, but their key myths shared a greatly similar pattern.

The Book of the Heavenly Cow / The Destruction of Mankind

The Book of the Heavenly Cow is a composition first recorded in several New Kingdom royal tombs, including those belonging to Tutankhamun, Seti I, and Ramesses II (Guilhou, 2010, p. 10). It is within this text that the Myth of the Heavenly Cow is recounted and unlike the scattered references of the myth previously mentioned, this story appears as a coherent narrative. Though recorded in the New Kingdom, the origins of the myth, like the Wandering Eye, may date to the earlier Middle Kingdom (Kelly Simpson, 2003, p. 289). The rather pleasant-sounding title may mislead readers to as the nature of its content; instead, a popular alternative name, 'The Destruction of Mankind', is more indicative of its theme.

The myth takes place ahead of time from that of the Wandering Eye when Ra has been ruling over creation for so long that his superior age has started to show. By this point, humankind had now been created, either from the tears of the Eye of Ra, or from the tears shed upon her return (Pinch, 2002, pp. 66-67). Noting the Creator's old age, and perhaps an inferred vulnerability, humanity had begun to turn against him, much to Ra's dismay.

The fact that Ra himself was afraid of human rebellion illustrates how the Egyptians viewed the delicate balance of the universe. It was vital for the king, and the priests on his behalf, to uphold cosmic order (*ma'at*) in the temples every day and night, to ensure the sun's rebirth each dawn (Wilkinson, 2000, p. 89). These enemies of Ra were therefore agents of chaos, who posed a very real threat to the Creator and his Creations. Moved to take serious action against this, Ra heeded his council's advice to dispatch his Eye to punish mankind for their treachery:

> *Send out your Eye that it may smite them for you, those who have conspired so wickedly.*
> *May it descend in the form of Hathor...*
> (*BHC*, 10-15; trans. Wente, 2003)

Hut-hor was a name for another Eye of Ra, who had been present from the beginning, as the Hand of Atum-Ra during creation. She wasted no time in seeing her father's will enacted and finding delight in this righteous vengeance she exclaims:

> *"I have overpowered mankind, and it was agreeable to my heart."*
> *And so, Sekhmet came into being.*
> (*BHC*, 14-15)

This translation could equally say, 'And so, *power* came into being', for the name *sḥm.t.* literally means 'power'. Through the act of justified divine retribution Hut-hor manifests her incarnate power and *becomes* 'the Powerful One'. This myth therefore explains how Sekhmet came into being and how her first action upon this earth was feasting upon the enemies of Ra.

Not only did Hut-hor-Sekhmet wreak vengeance on the evildoers, but she smote humankind indiscriminately. The myth continues, describing how, overcome with a taste for consuming human blood, nothing could stop her. Ra knew he would have to intervene if he was to prevent the entire annihilation of humanity between Sekhmet's jaws. The Netjeret could not be tamed, nor be reasoned with.

Ra had only one option; he would need to trick her into relenting and so ordered for the production of a substance made from red ochre and beer-mash, that would have an appearance and consistency 'just like human blood' (*BHC*, 15-25). Seven thousand jars of this thick, scarlet liquid were poured upon the land, flooding the fields of Egypt. This was much to Sekhmet's delight as she discovered it the following day:

> *The goddess set out in the morning, and so she found these (fields) inundated. Her face became delighted thereat. So she proceeded to drink, and it was just fine in her estimation.*
> *She returned so drunk that she had been unable to recognize mankind.*
> (*BHC*, 20-24)

Ra was so relieved when she stumbled home to the Delta, intoxicated from red beer, that he declared the introduction of an annual festival of drunkenness in her honour (Pinch, 2002, p. 75). This indicates that upon her appeasement, the Eye resumed her form as the beautiful Hut-hor. This return is a mirror image of the conclusion of the Wandering Eye, where Tefnut returned beautiful and amiable. To the ancient Egyptians, there was no problem with viewing Sekhmet, Tefnut, and Hut-hor, as both individual Netjerut *and* emanations of one another simultaneously.

The story moves on as Ra shares a somewhat sad reflection, that though he has regained humankind's respect through Sekhmet's intervention, it was achieved through the distribution of pain (*BHC*, 25-30). This sombre tone moves him to the decision to remove himself from the company of earth-dwelling Netjeru and humans and to return to the heavens. With the Eye of Ra no longer slaying humans indiscriminately, and perhaps saddened that their Creator wished to be apart from them, the supporters of Ra took up arms against his remaining enemies on earth. Though they intended to fight for righteousness and order, this introduced murder into the world of humans (*BHC*, 30-38). The myth ends with the sky Netjeret Nut transforming into a gigantic cow, allowing Ra to climb upon her back and be lifted towards the heavens, held up by Shu and the infinite stars (*BHC*, 40-44) – hence the overarching title 'The Myth of the Heavenly Cow'. Based on this title, the original intention appears to focus on why Ra left the earth and came to reside in the sky, rather than on the destruction of mankind.

Beyond a mythological explanation, Nadine Guilhou suggests two other functions for this myth. The first is its ritual function, indicated by the addition of rubrics in the text that outline ritual instructions to ensure the deceased king's ascension to the heavens, in imitation of Ra (Guilhou, 2010, p. 3). The second use for the myth is as an explanation of the seasons, which would make sense considering how the sun effects earth's agricultural cycles. In the heat of summer Egypt was parched, its crops fully harvested, and the agricultural plain thirsty for the greatly anticipated flood around July/August. This was understood to be a consequence of the fiery Eye of Ra burning down upon the earth. Guilhou suggests that the ochre-beer mixture that mythically flooded the land was a reference to the red silt that arrives with the inundation (Guilhou, 2010, p. 4); alternatively, this could be the red-earth that is made visible from the receding waters, prior to the flood (Richter, 2010, p. 158). Following the flood of the red waters, the intensity of the sun would decrease over the months ahead, suggestive of the Eye's appeasement after her blood feast (Roberts, 1995, p. 12). Betsy Bryan has suggested that lions moved away from the Valley and, representing the Wandering Eye, had to be encouraged to return, bringing the flood waters with them (Bryan, 2020).

The Myth of the Wandering Eye introduces the theme of

the Eye of Ra leaving the Creator vulnerable and returning to much jubilation. This mythic pattern is repeated in the Myth of the Destruction of Mankind where this time Ra calls upon his Eye to protect him during a crisis. The Eye does so with so much enthusiasm that Ra needs to pry her away from her prey by intoxicating her. She is welcomed home with great relief and celebration once again. Things are different the second time around, however. Though the myth suggests that Tefnut also wreaked havoc on her travels, a lioness needs to hunt after all, she is not brimming with devastating anger. When Huthor leaves to defend Ra, her fury is so great that she unleashes incarnate power itself, bringing Sekhmet into being.

Mythic Family

Sekhmet's role as a daughter of the sun Netjer is at this point very clear and will be explored in greater detail in Chapter 4, when discussing the role of the Eye(s) of Ra. This will naturally include any discussion of her sisters, which is mostly concerned with their syncretism with one another, rather than emphasising their familial tie.

Sekhmet is a member of the Memphite Triad, whose cult centre was the ancient city of Memphis, located just south of modern Cairo. The triad consisted of Sekhmet, the craftsman Netjer Ptah and their son, the child Netjer Nefertem (Pinch, 2002, p. 188). Ptah's history is very ancient and is attestable from Egypt's 1st Dynasty; he combined his skill as a craftsman with his role as a Creator and is instantly recognisable by his mummiform posture and the blue skull cap adorning his head (Wilkinson, 2003, pp. 123-125). The couple's child, Nefertem was an eternally youthful deity, who represented the primordial lotus from which the Solar Creator emerged at the dawn of creation (according to one myth). He could be depicted with a lotus upon his head, as Netjer of perfumes, or in leonine form identifying with his mother (Wilkinson, 2003, pp. 133-135). The triad are mentioned in a section of a New Kingdom love song:

The River is wine,
Ptah is its reeds,
Sekhmet is its lotus leaf,
Iadet is its lotus bud,
Nefertem is its Lotus flower...
(*Harris Papyrus 500*; Bryan, 2020)

It is not entirely clear why these three very different deities would be joined as a family triad. It may be that Sekhmet and Ptah became consorts due to the shared popularity of their cults in Memphis. Ptah was known to his followers as the craftsman of Creation; as such, he was connected to Ra and other Creator Netjeru, lending one reason as to why Sekhmet was affiliated with him. In their shared Memphite capital, they adopted the epithets of *nebet neb ankh-tawy,* or Lady and Lord of the Life of the Two Lands (Lange, 2016, p. 303; Wilkinson, 2003, p. 124). The combination of Sekhmet's healing powers and Ptah's creative skills could also suggest Nefertem's association with perfumes, which were a valued commodity to the Egyptians. Though less central to her cult, Sekhmet was also known as one of the mothers of the lion-headed war god Mahes, who shared her aggressive qualities (Pinch, 2002, p. 115).

A Contemporary Pagan Perspective

The idea that Sekhmet can be both an individual Netjeret and a syncretised form with Hut-hor (and other Netjerut) may either be difficult to comprehend, or relatively straightforward. Every individual Pagan today will adhere to their own theistic framework, according to tradition or personal gnosis. Regardless of how one views this, Egyptian mythology makes it clear that Sekhmet 'came into being' when Hut-hor manifested true rage within herself. This could be viewed in two ways; for example,

Sekhmet may have been born out of Hut-hor's rage and into an independent Netjeret. Alternatively, Hut-hor herself may have transformed into a vengeful aspect, with the title 'Sekhmet' or 'the Powerful One'.

It would not be at all surprising if the idea of a Netjeret slaughtering humankind and relishing in the taste of blood, is an unappealing concept for some people today; however, it is important for one to keep in mind the context of these actions. Why did Ra send his Eye to punish humanity in the first place? Why was she so furious? And who suffered from her wrath?

This all came about because the (human) enemies of Ra sought to destroy created life and the balance of *ma'at*. Though this may sound like an ambitious task for mere humans, it is not as incredulous as it may at first appear. In many ways, humankind are tiny creatures within a vast universe with little say in the machinations of the planets, the rising, and the setting of the sun. We cannot escape the inevitability of death and many of us still fall prey to diseases and illnesses; however, to say that we are insignificant upon this earth is misguided. All creatures leave their destructive impact, and the cumulative human impact is a considerable one. With that said, I have witnessed many discussions that cast all of humanity in the role of parasites upon the earth. I would like to contradict this with an acknowledgment that certain societies are more complicit in environmental destruction than others and that one's own is not representative of all others. I do not believe anyone would make such accusations towards many indigenous peoples, for example, and so sweeping accusations may cause harm in their generalisation.

Nevertheless, considerable damage to the environment, animals, and fellow humans is being done by many societies today. This fact serves as a poignant and sobering illustration of how widespread human activity can eat away at creation and life. Hut-hor sought to protect her father and Creation, and to do so she unleashed her power upon the world. We can read this myth as nature's attempt to maintain the balance of life, which at times comes at a harsh, painful cost. Natural disasters are an example of this and though not born from divine malice, innocent lives are claimed in their wake. This perspective is echoed by Anne Key, a woman who served as Sekhmet's Priestess in the Nevada desert. Key offers a refreshing acknowledgment of reconsidering Sekhmet's myth through a consciously 21st century lens, with her retelling of Sekhmet's anger directed towards people who, 'used without thought and waste the gifts of the land' (Key, 2011a, pp. 145-146). Key also, illustrates her interpretation of the myth as a social and ecological warning, though her hymn to Sekhmet:

We plundered the earth to serve our fear and pride
Wanting, taking, destroying with no regrets
We claimed mastership over the world wide
Our fears ensuring our own deaths with weapons and threats

Such injustice made Sekhmet's heart roar
Such greed and recklessness the Lioness abhorred...
(Key, 2011b, p. 86).

For many modern devotees of Sekhmet, her righteous rage is valued and considered to be necessary. Many of us, especially women, have been taught to hide their anger and suppress their feelings. Many of us have been taught to be quiet, compliant, and to people-please those in positions of power. Women of colour have been especially criticised for their anger and are frequently tone-policed. This is how we maintain hierarchies and power-over systems. How emancipating it must then feel to meet a Netjeret such as Sekhmet, who does not hold back, who openly expresses how she feels, and does not compromise her authenticity for the sake of pleasing others.

As Tefnut, she follows her own will and explores undiscovered places. As Hut-hor, and then Sekhmet, she adheres to her father's request to punish humanity, yet does so wilfully and to a greater extent than Ra had anticipated. In her ability to unleash disease and other unfavourable conditions, Sekhmet is not there to please anyone; however, this is not a demonstration of selfish disregard, for Sekhmet operates within the balance of *ma'at*. She upholds integrity, wilfulness, and is entitled to her anger.

It is unsurprising that the revival of Goddess Spirituality and contemporary Paganism came at a time of western counter-culturalism, protesting against our damaging environmental impact, against sexist oppression, racial discrimination, advocating LGBT+ rights, and so on. We have been taught to be afraid of anger, assuming that it is always related to violence, danger, and unsavoury people. However, it was anger which gave birth to the Stonewall riots; it was anger that has fronted women's marches; it is anger that leads the Black Lives Matter protests. If we don't get angry, we remain complicit in harmful systems; if we don't get angry, we allow the enemies of Ra to run the show, stamping over Creation. Releasing our anger does not *have* to be destructive, though it can be... Today's international landscape remains an arena of challenging the status quo and fighting against inequality. Many remain angry, *including* those who do not want to lose their privileged place benefitting from oppressive and exploitative systems; after all, why would they want these systems to fall if they benefit from them? We can transform this into something creative, replacing the old, tired, and harmful systems with something new, vital, and supportive. At other times, however, we need to actively dismantle and take down. Sekhmet is therefore the perfect Netjeret, archetype, symbol – however you see her – to bring forward transformative anger. We can all *become* Sekhmet.

Chapter 2

The Devouring Flame

Sekhmet could be succinctly described as 'an aggressive solar goddess who was the instrument of divine retribution' (Pinch, 2002, p. 187). Humankind were believed to have grown from the tears shed by the Eye of Ra; as such, during her rampage against those who opposed Ra, Sekhmet became the mother who consumes her own young (Pinch, 2002, p. 187). Sekhmet is a Netjeret very much associated with the merciful provision of healing, delivered through her priests; however, this healing would not be needed if she did not send her messengers of sickness and plague in the first place, for she is also known as 'the goddess of plague and disease' (Ritner, 2008, p. 53). Before discussing her healing aspects, I feel it is important to address her more destructive ones, as to the ancient Egyptians at least, Sekhmet was a Netjeret who brought aggressive protection or disease first, and healing second. I also believe it is important to avoid minimising this aspect of Sekhmet and favouring her more gentle aspects (as expressed through her sister Hut-hor). To do so would be to adhere to antiquarian interpretations that sought to discredit Sekhmet as a powerful aggressive female archetype.

It cannot be denied that according to ancient Egyptian sources, Sekhmet was a Netjeret who was feared as well as loved. This fear reflected the ancient understanding that sometimes nature is scary, uncomfortable, and heart-breaking. Some of the evidence discussed in this chapter may present Sekhmet in an unfavourable and frightening light; however, it is essential to keep in might the ancient context and the fact that Sekhmet was also greatly beloved. Ancient Egyptians shared their land with considerably dangerous animals, large and small. The coming of the flood was a destructive event and medicine was limited against the spread of diseases and the risks present during life events such as childbirth. All of these things operated within the natural balance of *ma'at*. The fact that hundreds of statues, amulets, and temple carvings depict Sekhmet is a testament to how the ancient Egyptians revered and loved her in conjunction with a sensible level of caution. Therefore, I advocate that we understand her destructive abilities according to the laws of nature and remembering that just as Sekhmet was Bringer of Pestilence, she was also Mistress of Life.

There are several destructive elements to Sekhmet which shall be outlined here: devouring heat, influence over harmful daemons, the spread of disease, involvement with warfare, and her association with the spilling of blood.

Disease & Daemons

Diseases, sickness, aches, pains, and nightmares could all be considered the result of malignant attack from different spiritual entities, from angry Netjeru or ancestors (*akhu*), to the condemned dead (*mutu*), and daemons. Whilst there was no single noun to categorise the final group, there are definite groupings and individual names for these liminal entities (Lucarelli, 2010, p. 1). Two groupings, the *khatiu* 'slaughterers' and the *shemaiu* 'wanderers' are known from the Old Kingdom *PT* and were the vengeful plague-bringers of Sekhmet and Bastet (Lucarelli, 2010, p. 3).

Sekhmet was known as the Dreaded Archer who loosened the 'Seven Arrows' against unfortunate victims; these were daemonic entities who spread infectious diseases (Pinch, 2002, p. 188; Pinch, 2006, p. 38). These Arrows of Sekhmet were particularly present at the start of the new year, following the flood, bringing devastating epidemics; they were believed to 'hurry through the land... [and] shoot their arrows from their mouth' (Borghouts, 1978, p. 23, no. 13; Roberts, 1995, p. 12). The 'Slaughterers of Sekhmet' were other emissaries of Sekhmet, who brought forth

22

other forms of torment to the living, particularly on unlucky days of the year, such as the days leading up to the New Year, when the river was low and rodents were more prevalent (Pinch, 2006, p. 38; Richter, 2010, p. 158). One particular spell takes a strong defensive approach against the Slaughterers of Sekhmet:

> For warding off the breath of the vexation, of the murderers and incendiaries, the emissaries off Sakhmet:
> Retreat, murderers! No breeze will reach me so that passers-by would pass on, to rage against my face. I am Horus who passes along the wandering demons of Sakhmet. Horus, sprout of Sakhmet! I am the Unique One, the son of Bastet - I will not die on account of you!
> (No. 15, Borghouts, 1978, p. 15)

Here, the person reciting the spell identifies with the Netjer Heru, who was known for surviving many dangers in his youth, thanks to the magic of his mother Aset. It is also significant that the spell describes 'the breath' of the daemons upon the breeze, alluding to air-borne plagues. The spell advocates that in addition to these words the reciter is to circumnavigate their house carrying a wooden club, so that they may not die from the plague that year.

Considering ancient living conditions – though the Egyptians were a comparatively hygienic culture – it is unsurprising that such a Netjeret would require deep respect and reverence. Her mythology provides a clear message of what happens when she is angered, and the effectiveness of propitiation and offerings of beer to cool her off. Prayers and spells involving Sekhmet were therefore a precautionary and preventative method, administered alongside hygiene observances.

Both Sekhmet and her emissaries were greatly feared, as well as revered. During the second and early first millennium BCE, a practice involving writing prayers on amulets was popular. These amuletic decrees would record the prophecies of an oracle, regarding a new-born child's fate, which would then be worn on their person as a means of protection against various harmful entities (Pinch, 2006, p. 117). Sekhmet and her son Nefertem were considered amongst these entities, as well as the angry aspects of several other Netjeru and daemons. Even Netjerut who were considered mostly benevolent could have a dangerous side too, such as the maternal and magical Aset (Amgad, 2018, p. 38).

Whether Arrow or Slaughterer these entities could be considered daemons, or in other words liminal entities between the worlds, not quite deities but certainly not mortal. Egyptian daemons were not always harmful, they could be helpful too, especially when called upon for protection. Apotropaic daemons can be seen on the ivory birth wands, often carrying snakes or knives in order to frighten away entities that would bring harm to the mother and infant (Pinch, 2006, pp. 40-41). During the Graeco-Roman period the daemon Tutu, who can appear as a sphinx wielding knives with a cobra for a tail, was amongst Sekhmet's followers and possessed great magic and protective capabilities (Raven, 2012, pp. 25-27). We should therefore avoid an anachronistic interpretation of daemons that we might have inherited from other religious traditions, although admittedly *some* features may be more familiar to what we might expect of daemons today.

Identifying if the allies of Sekhmet sought to cause harm or offer protection rather depended on whether or not the individual was found to have offended Sekhmet in some way. Not all illnesses or supernatural threats were the result of Sekhmet's will; however, this was indeed her and her allies' area of expertise. Sometimes even when the cause of ailments, such as a snake bite, or bad experiences such as falling off a ladder, could be easily explained through mundane means, it could still be considered the result of Sekhmet's anger (Pinch, 2006, p. 141). Egyptian medicine involved identifying the problem and potential causes, but also consideration for why it occurred, i.e. having displeased a Netjer or an angry deceased relative. Sometimes diseases would be interpreted as possession, therefore necessitating a kind of exorcism ritual containing medicinal elements (Pinch, 2006, p. 141).

Certainly, Sekhmet was a Netjeret who people prayed to when seeking healing and protection. But she was also one they sought protection *from*. Her wrath was so greatly feared, and her power so greatly respected, that people would wear amulets to entice her merciful side, especially at the New Year (Ritner, 2008, p. 51).

Blood

The connection between Sekhmet, blood, and disease is a fascinating one to consider. There is an initial and obvious connection which is immediately apparent in her form as a lioness. As a lioness she was a skilled predator who stalked, hunted, and feasted upon her prey, tearing great bloody chunks of flesh from their bodies. Seeing lions at mealtimes is quite a thing to witness... However, this dramatic violence is something very natural and necessary in the wild, though no less brutal. It is not surprising that ancient Egyptians, who paid great attention to the natural world, would have formed an image of the lioness Sekhmet who was eager to lap up blood in such a manner. Sekhmet is She of the blood-stained maw.

Perhaps building upon this observation, Sekhmet's connection with blood became a part of formal state religion. From the Old Kingdom onwards the ritual sacrifice and consuming of animal flesh was an important part of ancient Egyptian temple rituals (Ikram, 2012, p. 1). Priests of Sekhmet are often depicted in ritual butchery scenes, where animals were slaughtered and drained of their blood as a good sanitary practice (Ikram, 1995, p. 46). The *Litany of Sekhmet* highlights this role:

Eater of blood... for whom the desert animals have been killed on account of the fear which she inspires!...

(*The Litany of Sekhmet;* trans. Germond, 1981).

Priests of Sekhmet are shown in this role, regardless of the deity in receipt of the sacrifice (Capochichi, 2016, p. 50). Scholars have suggested that this practice demonstrates how the ancient Egyptians understood that diseases could be spread through blood and spoiled meat and that this could be mitigated by draining the blood before consumption. Based on this understanding of the relationship between blood and disease, Sandro Capochichi has suggested an alternative interpretation of the Myth of the Destruction of Mankind. According to his reading, Sekhmet, like a plague, ravages the land showing no mercy or exceptions; her fury is an epidemic spread by blood, echoed in the myth's flooding of the fields with a blood-imitating substance (Capochichi, 2016, p. 51). This sounds similar to a passage in the *Tale of Sinuhe*, in which the Egyptian author themself draws a comparison between the Pharaoh over-whelming foreign lands and that of Sekhmet plaguing the land with pestilence (*The Tale of Sinuhe,* 45-46; Kelly Simpson, 2003, p. 57).

Sekhmet therefore possesses both a mythical and ritual connection to blood. The Egyptian priests appear to have landed upon a compromise with Sekhmet: she would continue to enjoy feasting upon the blood of slaughtered animals and in exchange would protect Egypt against the spread of disease. Though this is not directly an act of healing, it demonstrates how Sekhmet was active in securing good-health and sanitary practices within the temple. Cleanliness in general was valued extremely highly in Egyptian temple culture, with ritual purity taken seriously by *wab* priests, (Teeter, 2011, p. 20).

The Devouring Flame

Sekhmet's destructive powers are put to apotropaic use in her role as an Eye Netjeret and protector of the Sun Netjer Ra (discussed further in Chapter 4). Sekhmet and Bastet's protective wrath made them dšr-jb, 'red of heart', emphasising the heat of their anger (Amgad, 2018, p. 41). With her mighty solar power, she would breathe fire upon her enemies, scorching them to annihilation (Wilkinson, 2003, p. 181). Ra not only summoned Sekhmet's ferociousness to quell the rebellion of mankind against him, but he summoned her during his daily battle with the chaos serpent 'Apep (Greek Apophis) whose name was too dangerous to be written without striking through it in some way. The Graeco-Roman *Bremner-Rhind Papyrus* (hereafter *BRP*) provides rituals and spells for *The Book of Overthrowing of 'Apep*, which describe how several deities assist Ra in defeating the chaos serpent each day. There is a lot of fiery imagery included in the ritual liturgy, including references which involve spitting fire:

> *The Magic Spell to be uttered when putting 'Apep on fire. Recite:*
> *Be thou utterly spat upon, O 'Apep…*
> *Be thou spat upon… Verily I have burned thee…*
> (*BRP*, 23.1-3; trans. Faulkner, 1937)

This connection between spitting and burning is a reference to Sekhmet as the Eye of Ra, the uraeus cobra rearing at Ra's brow, poised to spit venom into the eyes of her father's enemies. The cobra's venom was akin to the sensation of being burnt by fire. Sekhmet is referred to directly later in this ritual in 'The Second Chapter of Felling 'Apep the Foe of Ra':

> *The Eye of Ra shall appear against you, his might shall have power over you, his Eye shall have power over you, it shall consume you and chastise you in its name of 'Devouring Flame'; it shall have power over you in its name of Sakhmet; ye shall fall to its blast, and fierce is the flame of fire which comes forth…*
> (*BRP*, 25.2-4)

Here, her epithet 'Devouring Flame' is quite appropriate, seen as scorching solar fire decimating those beneath her gaze, and the flames of cobra-venom with the power to burn away the recipient's life... Thus, as the Eye of Ra and the sun Netjer's defender, Sekhmet is not only a hunting lioness, she is also manifest as the rearing cobra. In many statues of Sekhmet that remain today, one can see the uraeus upon her brow, uniting these two forms and combining both the beneficent qualities of the sun and the devastating properties of a cobra's venom. Some statues, such as one located in the Karnak temple Mut precinct, are crowned with a circle of uraeii, poised to spit venomous-fire in every direction.

War

As defender of Ra, Sekhmet was the defender of the Pharaoh by association. This not only meant in his day-to-day life, but also in the dangers posed by real or theoretical participation in war and battle. She was the poised cobra who defended the sun Netjer each day, and the Myth of the Destruction of Mankind illustrates what happens when the power of Sekhmet is unleashed upon the world. She was therefore an indispensable ally to have on one's side on the battlefield. By wearing her as the uraeus upon his brow, the Pharaoh invoked the Eye Netjeret's protection and the Eye symbolised his unrivalled power in battle (Wilkinson, 2003, p. 181). At this point we can recall the gruesome scene from the predynastic *Battlefield palette*, where the ruler-as-lion tears his human foes apart. Perhaps this was Sekhmet imbuing the ruler with her terrible might, such as she continues to do centuries later?

Sekhmet comes to the Pharaoh's defence as a keen archer, referring to her dispensation of the aforementioned Seven Arrows. It was said that a single arrow released by Sekhmet had the power to slay thousands (*Songs in honour of Senwosret III,* 1.7; Kelly Simpson, 2003, p. 303). Sekhmet embodies the uncompromising female warrior archetype. She is both terrifying and magnificent in her battle fury. An inscription from Abu Simbel records how during a battle, Ramses II 'made heaps into corpses, like Sekhmet raging during a plague' (Amgad, 2018, p. 38). Mut-Sekhmet's violent assistance is likewise invoked by the female Pharaoh Hastshepsut, during a festival of drunkenness:

May you awaken propitiated;
May the pestilence which is upon your mouth and the slaughter
which is upon your lips awaken...
May you judge this matter which the King of Egypt [Maatkare]
has spoken to you;
O Sakhmet, may you be powerful of heart. Be powerful indeed over
those who hate her.
May you do this matter which she has spoken to you.
(Bryan, 2020)

Thus, Hatshepsut calls upon Sekhmet, praying that she look upon her favourably, and unleash destruction upon her enemies. In this way, Sekhmet's aggression is much appreciated and protects the Egyptians from their enemies (both mundane and spiritual). One of her divine sons, Mahes, shared her leonine form and inherited his mother's interest in warfare (Wilkinson, 2003, p. 178).

A Contemporary Pagan Perspective

I have chosen to discuss Sekhmet's violent nature prior to her protective or healing roles for two reasons. First, many prayers and spells which provide evidence of her healing powers suggest that they are in response to ailments, rather than methods of prevention; therefore, it makes sense to address her role as the cause of such things before remedial action can be implemented. And second, I wanted to balance the scales in terms of modern interpretations of her healing nature. Sekhmet is an increasingly popular Netjeret amongst contemporary Pagans, with many finding comfort, healing, strength, and safety between her paws. It is highly likely that Sekhmet has continued to change and develop with the passing centuries. But I also believe it is important to remember Sekhmet's Egyptian context and not to shy away from aspects that might make us more uncomfortable. It would be a disservice to Sekhmet and her ancient worshippers to bury her role as a war Netjeret, or the dispenser of disease and daemonic entities. As aforementioned, the ancient Egyptians actively sought to protect themselves *from* Sekhmet, as well as to appease and worship her.

How do contemporary Pagans negotiate worshipping – or 'working with' - a Netjeret who thirsts for blood, who brings disease, and who is more than happy to set loose angry daemons on those who anger her, or harm her devotees? Sekhmet's behaviour is closely tied to the ways of nature. As a lioness, her thirst for blood and merciless killing of prey is within the balance of nature and is quite different from the deliberate destruction that humans are capable of (although, admittedly felines are known to toy with their prey before the kill...). Her connection to blood is also a lesson in cleanliness and taking precautions against disease. Sekhmet's place in the temple butchery can represent how she takes an active role in ensuring her worshippers remain safe from the threat of illness caused by poor hygiene and unsafe practice.

In terms of blood specifically, Sekhmet can also be insatiable when blood is provided as an offering, and so we might choose to avoid such offerings today. Instead, we can imitate the myth and offer her beer, or libations which may appear blood-like. Considering how ancient rituals to Sekhmet aimed for her appeasement, offering beer is most suitable. Alternatively, one might feel that real blood remains a significant offering today, in which case it might be sourced from an abattoir or butchery. Raw meat can also be offered. I would not advocate sacrificing one's own blood in this instance, for it is a very un-Egyptian practice and would cross the boundaries of ritual purity so deeply adhered to by the ancient Egyptians. I believe honouring this offers due respect to these ancestors, though some may disagree.

In terms of her role as bringer of disease, no matter how hygiene-conscious we may be, or how many offerings we may give, we all get sick at some point in life. Disease and illness are an inevitable part of the human experience, although the level of superstition we place on this today may be less so compared to the ancient world. Do we credit Sekhmet for contemporary disasters and subsequent loss of life? Some Pagans will vehemently say no, others, may think differently. Perhaps the Netjeru are deeply interconnected with scientific explanations? If Sekhmet is the bringer of disease, there is no reason she cannot achieve this according to the laws of nature.

The connection to daemons is not unique to Sekhmet, for daemons regularly interacted with numerous other Netjeru. Again, this is an area worth exploring further than I can do so here. At the very least it is vital to know that we should not view ancient Egyptian daemons through an Abrahamic religious lens. Daemons are inclusive of spirits found in both the natural landscape, and the other worlds; it incorporates a large, vague category of liminal entities. Sekhmet may send them to help you on her behalf, or to teach you a lesson. This is so for many of the Netjeru, though Sekhmet is particularly inclined towards this daemonic assistance.

Perhaps most importantly I want to emphasise that Sekhmet's greatest healing comes from her destructive nature. She is an aggressive defender of *ma'at*, whose powers centre upon her ability to fiercely protect Ra and his creations. She is the one to call upon during dire situations, from combating chronic or life-threatening illnesses, or when undergoing serious surgery, to invoking her to prevent or end traumatising experiences of abuse and violence. It is essential that we do not minimise or demonise righteous rage and specifically female anger. Outdated misogynistic interpretations of Sekhmet perpetuate the idea that as an angry bloodthirsty female deity, she is one to be feared and who must be 'pacified' through intoxication rituals. Though some ancient sources may suggest this view, it is important to remember the historical context, but also to bear in mind that modern readings have often been influenced by outdated androcentric narratives.

Therefore, we should celebrate and respect Sekhmet's role as the Devouring Flame, bringer of plague and pestilence, and subduer of the enemies of Ra. She is absolutely essential to the balance of *ma'at,* and is a Netjeret whose aggressive nature and burning fire we absolutely need during our darkest hours...

Chapter 3

The Great Healer

It has been explained how Sekhmet was a Netjeret responsible for the spread of plague and pestilence across the land. The heat of the summer sun, prior to the inundation was believed to be the hot breath of this lioness Netjeret, a breath which also spread airborne diseases. Due to this overwhelming power, Sekhmet was also the one most able to retract this fate and could be prayed to for healing. As such, she became the patron of medicine, whose priests were specialists in both healing medicine and magic (Pinch, 2002, p. 188). All Egyptian Netjeru possessed two opposing personalities, for all could be beneficent or destructive, though some often veered more towards one or the other. Sekhmet's destructive power was significant and she was one of the more aggressive of Ra's daughters; however, her ability to heal was also great, rivalled only by the magical abilities of Aset. Both Aset and Sekhmet could be considered *weret-hekau*, or Great of Magic. To the Egyptians magic was most often needed in times of crisis, relating to illness, poisonous animal bites, or naturally dangerous events such as childbirth.

Priests of Sekhmet & Healing

One of the best surviving examples of an ancient Egyptian medical text is now known as the

Edwin Smith Papyrus; dating to around 1900 BCE, the papyrus contains forty-eight medical cases. Within this text priests of Sekhmet are listed amongst those responsible for conducting the listed medical procedures (Aziz, 2018, p. 36). Priests of Sekhmet often held dual titles identifying them as both priests and doctors, such as in the case of Wenen-Nefer, who lived during the Old Kingdom and held the title of '*wab* priest of Sekhmet', as well as *sehedj sunu*, 'inspector of physicians' (Aziz, 2018, p. 36; Pinch, 2006, p. 53). Case 1 of the *Edwin Smith Papyrus* states that both priests of Sekhmet and physicians could check for a patient's pulse:

> *Now if the priests of Sekhmet or any physician put his hands (or) his fingers [upon] the head, upon the back of [the] head, upon the two hands, upon the pulse, upon the two feet, [he] measures [to] the heart because its vessels are in the back of the head and in the pulse...*
>
> *(Edwin Smith Papyrus, case 1; trans. Breasted, 1930, p. 104)*

The reason for such dual-affiliations may have been because, as Sekhmet was the bringer of disease, her priests were believed to have been the people best equipped to appease her and to convince her to retract such afflictions. Having knowledge of diseases and the like would have been essential to their full understanding of Sekhmet and would therefore lead her priests to possessing transferable skills for a medical occupation. As well as healing people from diseases Sekhmet would have also been invoked to support her doctor-priests conducting serious medical procedures, such as surgeries, as well as at times overseeing the healing of livestock and other animals.

Doctors were known as *sunu* and priests of Sekhmet were called *wab Sekhmet* (Ritner, 2008, p. 53). The former title, *sunu* could be held by priests as well as Netjeru and Netjerut; however, the evidence has yielded very few women with this title from ancient Egypt (Pinch, 2006, p. 54). There is a significant lack of references to priestesses dedicated to Sekhmet, or at least women who held such a title. Priestesses of other Netjerut are attested during the Old Kingdom but were increasingly uncommon as time went on; by the New Kingdom, women usually took on the role of temple chantress, *shemayet*, instead (Teeter, 2011, p. 27). Pinch suggests that this was due to lower literacy rates amongst women and the taboo of menstruation in terms of ritual purity, although this does not explain the reason for the gradual change, considering their existence in earlier periods (Pinch, 2006, p. 56). Nevertheless, considering the fact that playing music to pacify the Eyes of Ra was a central religious ritual, we may safely understand that the role of a *shemayet* was indeed a significant one.

In addition to some priests also working as doctors and physicians, they could also hold titles pertaining to magical practitioners, such as Herishefnakht who was a master physician as well as an *imy-r hekau,* 'overseer of magicians' (Aziz, 2018, p. 37). Magic and medicine were often deeply interconnected in ancient Egypt. The role of a *sau* (after *sa,* meaning 'protection') was one held by men *and* women and referred to a person who specialised in the production and use of protective amulets (Pinch, 2006, p. 56). Women who took up the part time role of midwife could also be considered *sau.* Amulet-makers are listed amongst other medical practitioners, such as *sunu* and *wab Sekhmet*; though not directly involved in her cult, the provision of amulets by amulet-makers who often invoked her protection or repelled her anger, suggests that some magical affiliation between the *sau* and Sekhmet must have existed (Ritner, 2008, p. 53).

The New Year was considered an especially dangerous time where the risk of disease was high, owing to an increase in rodents, intense heat, and low food awaiting the flood. The coming of the inundation, though celebrated, was equally destructive when it came in too high, overwhelming settlements. At this time, priests of Sekhmet and associated magical practitioners took preventative measures, seeking to appease Sekhmet and mitigate the destruction (Pinch, 2002, p. 188). This included healing amulets known as *sa-en-sehetep-Sekhmet*, protection spells, and appeasement rituals (outlined in Chapters 6 and 7). In addition to controlling her seven emissaries, Sekhmet also had influence over thirty-six Netjeru who each presided over a set of ten days dividing the year; thus, when appeased, she would ensure year-long protection (Raven, 2012, p. 22).

One text recorded on a piece of graffiti records how a Herishefnakht laid his hands upon a patient to identify the source of their ailment:

The priest of Sekhmet Herishefnakht says: I used to be the overseer of the pure priests of Sekhmet, overseer of magicians, and chief physician of the King, who daily reads the scroll... who lays his hand on the patient and thereby acquires knowledge about him, who is an expert in examining by means of the hand.
(*Quarries of Hatnub, graffito* 15; Raven, 2012, p. 29)

It is ambiguous here whether the laying on of hands refers to a physical examination only or alludes to a spirito-magical practice of sensing afflictions. There are many records of spells that are aimed at specific ailments, whether illnesses, accidents, or incidences of spiritual phenomena (i.e. spirit possession, or hauntings). The spells that do mention Sekhmet or her emissaries by name typically do so to ward away her destructive influence rather than to invoke her protection (though some do exist for the latter; Borghouts, 1978, p. 2, no. 5). Perhaps it was believed that owing to their devotional connection to Sekhmet, she was inclined to listen to her priest-magician-doctors when they asked her to desist.

A particularly famous case of invoking Sekhmet's healing powers is suggested through the existence of hundreds of statues in her likeness dating to the reign of Amenhotep III in the New Kingdom. Some scholars have suggested that Amenhotep had become seriously ill and, in an attempt to save his life, he commissioned over 700 statues of Sekhmet to appease her (Aziz, 2018. p. 39). These are now scattered amongst the world's museums and are discussed in greater detail in Chapter 6.

However, it is important to bear in mind that not all scholars agree that this was the intended use of the statues (Bryan, 2020).

Mistress of Life

One of Sekhmet's epithets was 'Mistress of Life'; with command over the balance of sickness and health she indeed held the fates of people's lives within her hands (Wilkinson, 2003, p. 181). As succinctly outlined by Sophia Aziz, 'simply by withholding her destructive potency... she bestowed life' (Aziz, 2018, p. 35).

As Mistress of Life, Sekhmet's beneficent qualities could be witnessed. An exquisite golden aegis and *menat* (a ceremonial necklace with a large counterweight at the back), now resides in the Walters Art Museum; on it is an image depicting a nurturing aspect of Sekhmet nursing Heru as a child. This item may have functioned as an amulet or given as a votive offering to Sekhmet (Walters Art Museum, no. 57.540). This aegis depicts Sekhmet as a mother figure, bestowing life-giving milk to Heru, and the Pharaoh by association. This is reminiscent of the aforementioned *PT* spell 248, where Sekhmet and Shezmetet conceive and give birth to the Pharaoh. Bastet is a Netjeret often shown surrounded by kittens and was believed to protect the home. There are ancient sculptures that depict lionesses with their cubs also. Lionesses are fierce protectors of their young and as an Eye Netjeret Sekhmet was equally protective of those under her care. It should be noted, however, that despite this maternal side, it would be misleading to identify her as a 'Mother Goddess', for this was not her ancient role. Other Eyes of Ra, such as Mut (pronounced *Moot*), would be much more suited to this identification (though by no means limited to it).

Sekhmet's role as Mistress of Life is also evident in her full-size statues that now populate museums around the world. Her breasts are adorned with carved rosettes and her throne is decorated by papyrus stalks. *Harris Papyrus 500* describes Sekhmet as the 'lotus leaf' and her son, Nefertem is the 'lotus flower' from which the creator emerges, according to one creation myth (Bryan, 2020). Such references to vegetation, coupled with her sun disc headdress, portray her as a Netjeret of life-giving sunlight. Though Sekhmet certainly represented the burning heat of the summer sun, the sun was also the face of the creator, shining down on Egypt and sustaining life.

A Contemporary Pagan Perspective

Sekhmet as Mistress of Life & Goddess of Healing today

Though modern devotees of Sekhmet recognise and honour her destructive abilities, Sekhmet is deeply loved for her maternal protection and significant healing powers. Her motherly approach, however, differs from other Netjerut, focusing on offering fierce compassion and encouraging us to face our fears with courage, burning away that which does not serve us. Though there are scant ancient references to Sekhmet in association with fertility, according to local Egyptian folklore and contemporary Pagan experiences, through engaging with her statues, Sekhmet appears to be willing to respond to prayers from those desiring to conceive children (Vaughan, 2011, p. 69). This does actually make a lot of sense, as if Sekhmet has influence over one's health, she must also have power over the physical body; furthermore, if she can take away life, she can also bestow it. As a Netjeret associated with blood, some have also interpreted this to include menstrual and womb blood, which likewise flows with the currents of both life and death (Vaughan, 2011, p. 71).

Those whose careers are involved in medicine and the health of humans or animals may feel a connection to Sekhmet and her ancient priesthood. Though scientific enquiry should be prioritised, Sekhmet may be an appropriate Netjeret to call upon when learning about various diseases and illness, and when seeking to overcome them. It remains essential that medical professionals understand the science behind illnesses, including the cause, in order to understand how to heal them; to me, this involves understanding Sekhmet at work.

Sekhmet is a Netjeret to turn to when serious afflictions arise. Other Netjeret, such as Aset could be preferred when seeking soothing remedies, or navigating the risks of pregnancy and birth, and venomous bites; however, calling upon Sekhmet is ideal when one needs to take an aggressive stance against health concerns.

Sekhem & Seichim healing

A quotation offered in this chapter spoke of a priest of Sekhmet laying his hands upon a patient to identify the source of their affliction. Evidence such as this may prompt some contemporary healing practitioners to think of various other traditions that teach healing through energetic touch. One such tradition, inspired by Sekhmet's healing powers is *Sekhem* or *Seichim* healing. Conceptually these appear to be the same, with the difference mostly residing in their spelling preference and by the individuals who claim to have founded (or re-discovered) the practice. *Sekhem* was founded by a woman named Helen Belót in the 1990's (sekhem.com.au). *Seichim* was founded by Patrick Zeigler at the start of the 1980's, following his overnight stay in the Great Pyramid of Giza (all-love.com/ourstory). Pamela Christine Evans MBE, who is a trained *Seichim* Master and teacher, has kindly contributed her explanation of *Seichim*:

Whilst laying in meditation in the granite sarcophagus, he [Patrick] saw and felt the whirling energy of a presence that appeared above him in the pattern of a figure of eight. The energy entered his heart chakra and then the whole of his being. Patrick describes that he felt filled with a Divine energy of love that stayed with him the whole night. When he left the pyramid in the morning, he discovered that the whole of his body was covered in a strange white dust.

I had the pleasure of spending a retreat weekend with Patrick who confirmed my feelings that the Goddess Sekhmet is linked with what Patrick currently calls SKHM, Sekhem and Seichim healing which is taught worldwide.

In ancient Egypt, Sekhmet was considered to be the Mother of the Gods and was known as The Great One of Healing. Her magician-priests were the greatest of all healers and her son, Nefar-Tem, the God of Physicians.

"Seichim" is an Egyptian word meaning living light energy. It is also known as the "power of powers" and allows you to heal from the Divine Source to the physical body through the aura and etheric body.

Pamela Christine Evans MBE *Seichim Master Teacher* https://peacemala.org.uk

Today many *Sekhem/Seichim* practitioners can be found, with online resources offering teaching and consultations. This healing tradition is founded upon the concept of Sekhmet as the Netjeret of healing *par excellence*, whose name embodies the energetic power of healing itself. Practitioners claim that *Sekhem/Seichim* healing is an ancient Egyptian healing practice and often refer to the *Book of the Dead* as its source. As aforementioned, a quote provided in this chapter may lead readers to believe that this is an ancient practice. Whether it is genuinely ancient or not, the power known by the ancient Egyptians as *sekhem* certainly is for contemporary Pagans and/or practitioners. Tuning in to *sekhem* appears to be a tangible way for many contemporary devotees to connect with Sekhmet's healing power, aside from the avenue of destruction that she also offers.

Healing through destruction

Many devotees of Sekhmet today (as well as devotees of other aggressive deities) hold the view that Sekhmet can offer great healing through her destructive powers. I choose to discuss this interpretation here as it appears to be a decidedly modern approach to Sekhmet, rather than one clearly identifiable in the ancient evidence. Nicki Scully's book *Sekhmet: Transformation in the Belly of the Goddess,* offers up a journey with Sekhmet, whereby the lioness Netjeret consumes that which does not serve her devotees, so that they may be transformed. Sekhmet is presented here as a Netjeret to whom one offers their fears, past traumas, their negative habits and behaviours, and who subsequently devours them as she devoured the enemies of Ra; furthermore, she ingests the supplicant in the process, digesting them within her belly, until they themselves emerge transformed, anew, and healed (Scully, 2017). Sekhmet's flames are also considered to be the key to regeneration:

Her passion heated in the red hot flames of time, change and transformation...
She calls all into her loving heart: "Come to me, and bring me your sorrow and your tears. Together we will walk through the fire of transformation."
(Stirling, 2011, p. 67).

This concept is evocative of destructive acts of nature, such as wildfires which devastate landscapes, but result in fertile soils beneath the ashes. Likewise, in an Egyptian context, the annual inundation would sweep across the Nile Valley, destroying settlements and flooding the land; this destruction sated the thirsty earth and left behind fertile fields and lush foliage. It may therefore be quite appropriate to consider Sekhmet's destruction in this way, for indeed, she was the primary defender of Ra and acted in accordance with the laws of *ma'at*, rather than intending to destroy without meaning.

Sekhmet is the defender of justice and those who have been wronged. As such, one might face times when recovering from trauma is needed. Sekhmet's aggressive healing can take the form of one *becoming* Sekhmet to channel righteous rage, or seeking to exact justice against one's perpetrators, as well as the process of recovery from physical and emotional forms of abuse. It is in these latter forms that Sekhmet as the Great Healer is most visible, offering healing through destruction. Heeding righteous rage can be a healing act that we need not fear or suppress.

Chapter 4

The Eyes(s) of Ra

So far, this book has made numerous references to Sekhmet as the Eye of Ra and to several other Eye Netjerut. This chapter aims to focus on the meaning of this title and to explore these other Eyes more closely, as they all have relevance to the mythology and worship of Sekhmet. Sekhmet's form as a lioness is well-known and celebrated; however, she is also connected to the cobra. Cobras are worn by Sekhmet, either as an uraeus at her forehead, or circling the entirety of her headdress, as is the case for a statue of Sekhmet from the temple of Mut in Karnak (Bryan, 2020). Visually the Eye was symbolised either by the *Udjat* Eye (see fig. 5) or by the rearing cobra. *Uraeus* is the Greek word for the original Egyptian *iaret,* meaning 'the one who rears up', describing how a cobra stands erect when ready to attack (Pinch, 2002, p. 199). This is often seen at the brow of Netjeru, Pharaohs, and queens, for their protection (fig. 2).

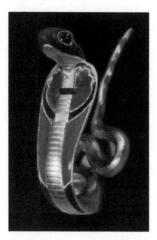

*Figure 2. Uraeus cobra, separated from original crown
(Egyptian Museum Cairo, JE46694)*

The Sun and the Moon

There can be much confusion between identifying the Eye of Ra and the Eye of Heru (or Eye of Horus) as in Egyptian iconography these both appear identical. Sometimes they are also described very similarly in the ancient texts. Whilst they can be considered two separate things with some mythic variations, there remains considerable overlap; for example, in *PT* 689 the Eyes of Ra and Heru are *both* identified with the uraeus cobra (Richter, 2010, pp. 157-158).

The Eye of Ra is predominantly connected to the sun. Netjerut, such as Sekhmet and Hut-hor are often crowned by the sun disc and are very obviously aligned with fiery associations. An image of Hut-hor in the temple of Dendera depicts her as the embodiment of the midday sun in the sky, with her anthropomorphic form contained within the orb of the sun as part of the hieroglyph *akhet,* meaning horizon (Bryan, 2020). Some Eyes of Ra, such as Tefnut, could take on a lunar aspect, especially in relation to the Myth of the Wandering Eye. This is reflected by the festival celebrating the Eye's return taking place on the full moon to represent the Eye's full visibility in the sky (Richter, 2010, p. 158). This lunar association is also evident in myths relating to the Eye of Heru specifically. In Heru's mythology, as a child he underwent various episodes of suffering poisonous animal attacks and being healed by his mother Aset (as recorded on the *Metternich Stela*; translation by Scott, 1951). As an adult, during his battles with his uncle Sutekh, Sutekh tore out one of Heru's eyes; this time, Hut-hor came to his aid, healing the eye with her bovine milk. This story of regeneration was used to explain the waxing and waning of the moon in the sky each month (Pinch, 2002, p. 132).

These solar and lunar associations led to each Eye representing one or the other: thus, the right Eye was the sun and the left Eye the moon (Darnell, 1995, p. 35). The connection between the Eye and healing, combined with the fact that the Eye hieroglyph was iconographically identical to that of Ra's, meant that both could be used interchangeably in healing rituals, spells, and amulets, and therefore could be used in the healing and protective works of Sekhmet.

The Eye as Protector

The earliest hint of the Eye of Ra belongs to the *PT* and equates the king with the sun, which is both Ra's Eye and Ra himself; with this, the spell mentions the Eye upon Hut-hor's brow which is reborn each day (*PT* 405). This could refer to the later myth from the *Book of the Heavenly Cow*, where Hut-hor – or Nut – lifts the sun disc, Ra, between her horns and into the sky, leaving the world of humanity behind (Richter, 2010, p. 157). According to the mythology surrounding Ra's Eye, the first Eye was created and placed upon Ra's brow to watch over him and his creations. He created his second Eye when the first wandered away from him as he needed the Eye's protection, and in some versions because he needed her to retrieve the original Eye (*CT* 76). This reflects how from the beginning Ra intended his Eye to remain close to the creator, watching over creation as the solar disc, and providing defensive protection.

The protection offered by the Eye of Ra was present both in a literal and a personified sense, clearly expressed in a royal hymn to Ra from the 11th Dynasty:

My protection is the red glow of your eye.
(Stela MMA 13.182.3, 1. 6; trans. Allen, 2007)

The orthography of this line is written without the determinative sign for the Netjeret, perhaps indicating that it is Ra's literal eye that is glowing red and providing protection. It is likely that this was an intentional pun, as the Egyptian viewer would have been aware of the mythic meaning of Ra's Eye; it would therefore have been obvious that this has a double meaning, both as Ra's protective gaze, and that of his Eye daughter, who offered protection through blazing red fire. This line, and the appearance of uraeii on royal and divine headdresses, reflects how the Eye extended her protection not only to Ra, but to all those who are responsible for maintaining the creator's order.

In addition to representing the creator's bodyguard, as it were, the Eye was also active in both defence and attack. Hut-hor responded without question when Ra summoned her to protect creation from the human adversaries who sought to disrupt it. It is through the active form of protection, through attack, that Sekhmet comes into being. Sekhmet is distinct from other entities who protect through defence, or through scaring enemies away through their threatening presence. Sekhmet needs little excuse to unleash her destruction. Indeed, by the New Kingdom she appears to be considered one of the most aggressive aspects of the Eye of Ra (Pinch, 2002, p. 188).

Nevertheless, this blood-thirsty eagerness remains within the confines of order. Sekhmet is a primary defender of *ma'at*, the concept of order and balance in the universe. When we consider her angry destructive aspects, it is therefore important to remember them in the context of a Netjeret whose ferocity is primarily aimed at defending creation, by whatever means possible (and yes, for Sekhmet, this may include violence). The concept of *ma'at* was also personified as a Netjeret herself, who by the New Kingdom adopted the epithet, 'daughter of Ra' identifying her as an Eye of Ra (Wilkinson, 2003, p. 150). Ma'at was not associated with the protective aggression usually expected from Eye Netjerut. Instead, she was more like other Eyes such as Aset, whose protection was offered through the use of magic, or *heka*. Sekhmet and Ma'at are therefore linked as Eyes of Ra, with Sekhmet operating within the confines of Ma'at's order, and seeking to uphold this at all costs.

As the great protectress of Ra, Sekhmet stood at the prow of his solar barque to face the chaos serpent 'Apep, who threatened creation on the seventh and twelfth hours of the night, jeopardising the coming sunrise (Pinch, 2002, pp. 107, 188). In *The Book of Overthrowing 'Apep*, Sekhmet appears as the Devouring Flame and the Glorious Eye, who burns 'Apep with the touch of her finger and 'the fiery breath of her mouth', and who 'cuts out his heart' (*BRP* 25.2-4, 27.8-9, 15-17). In temples, priests would contribute to this nightly battle by performing rituals against 'Apep, involving the creation of diminutive models of him and burning or smashing them (Pinch, 2002, p. 108).

Identification with other Eyes

There are several other Netjerut who were identified as Eyes of Ra. More or less any Netjeret who was associated with felines could take on aspects of the Eye; in addition to this, to some degree all female Netjerut were associated with cobras, as indicated by the cobra, or uraeus, appearing as a determinative hieroglyph at the end of many Netjerut names. There are, however, certain Netjerut were more commonly associated with the Eye of Ra, and Sekhmet specifically, than others.

According to the Heliopolitan version of creation, Atum-Ra first created Shu and Tefnut, making Tefnut the first Wandering Eye and one who also primarily took the form of a lioness. Alternative versions report that Ra-Atum united with his Hand, which became known as a manifestation of Hut-hor, and so arguably Hut-Hor came first. Discussion of Hut-hor could occupy an entire volume itself, as her cult was extremely popular across Egypt and throughout ancient Egyptian history. Though she was commonly known as the patron of music, dancing, sexuality, and festivities, Hut-hor also had close ties to birth, guiding people to the afterlife, and as the rearing cobra, was poised to shoot flaming venom at any who threatened those dear to her heart (Pinch, 2002, pp. 137-139). She was popular amongst the elite and common people alike. Hut-hor was not typically associated with lion imagery, however, and was more deeply connected to bovines and serpents. It is from her, following Ra's instructions to smite humanity during their rebellion, that Sekhmet came into being. The two are therefore inextricably linked and could be seen as two different sides of the same Netjeret. Indeed, just as Sekhmet has 'Seven Arrows', Hut-hor has 'Seven Hut-hors' (commonly known today as the Seven Hathors; Pinch, 2006, pp. 37-38). Nevertheless, ancient Egyptian religion allowed for multiple co-existing truths, and so, whilst this interpretation is accurate, it is *also* true that the two Netjerut were distinct and independent as well.

In the same way, Bastet and Sekhmet are also intimately associated. Until the end of 2000 BCE, Bastet was frequently shown-lion headed, but after this date she became increasingly associated with cats instead; furthermore, both she and Sekhmet were considered mothers of the lion Netjer, Mahes (Pinch, 2002, p. 115). Sekhmet's beneficent nature is less obvious than that of Bastet's, whose benevolent side is often emphasised in contrast to Sekhmet. This is humorously demonstrated in one Egyptian text comparing married women to gentle cats like Bastet and enraged lionesses like Sekhmet; (Capel & Markoe, 1997, p. 136). This is also suggested in depictions of Bastet in common association with kittens. However, despite such references to Bastet's nurturing side, she certainly also appeared as the terrifying Eye of Ra. Spells describe the 'Slaughterers of Bastet' who dispensed plague just as mercilessly as the Slaughters of Sekhmet. Previously provided is a quotation from a spell to ward off the emissaries of Sekhmet, which includes pronouncing, 'I am... the son of Bastet - I will not die on account of you' (Borghouts, 1978, p. 15, no. 15). Another commands:

Let your murderers retreat, Bastet... your breeze will not reach me... I am the jubilated one, oh son of Bastet!
(No. 20, Borghouts, 1978, p. 17).

These suggest that such daemons, who bring plague upon the winds will not cause harm to those affiliated with Bastet. Bastet will not harm her offspring and will protect them instead. Despite these similarities it is important to note that both Netjerut remain distinct and can be seen rather like twin sisters, sharing traits yet maintaining individuality.

Another Eye Netjeret closely associated with Sekhmet is Mut. Mut was the consort of the Netjer, Amun, and shared a cult centre with him in Thebes; her earliest depictions date to the Middle Kingdom (Wilkinson, 2003, pp. 153-154). Her name translates to 'mother' and she was considered a mother of the Netjeru, and the Pharaoh. Egyptian queens would identify with her in this way, as the mothers of the future rulers. By the New Kingdom, Mut became identified with the Eye of Ra and started to appear in leonine form, as well as anthropomorphically; this is perhaps due to her growing identification with Sekhmet, who she is equated with directly in an inscription on one of Amenhotep III's many statues of Sekhmet (Capel & Markoe, 1997, p. 136). Mut's cult began to take on more aspects of Sekhmet's mythology and by the New Kingdom's 18th Dynasty, the rituals related to the Eye myth started to take place regularly in her temple (Capel & Markoe, 1997, p. 136). As an Eye Netjeret, she could also take the appearance of other Eye's, such as Hut-hor, appearing human-headed and crowned with bovine horns cradling the sun disc (Wilkinson, 2003, p. 155). It is therefore often difficult to ascertain who is represented in the absence of hieroglyphic labels.

Likewise, Pakhet is an aggressive lioness huntress attested from the Middle Kingdom, who is almost indistinguishable from Sekhmet on reliefs, except from the labelling hieroglyphs. Her name means "she who scratches", which is echoed in a *CT* spell describing her thus:

I have appeared as Pakhet the Great,
whose eyes are keen and whose claws are sharp,

the lioness who sees and catches by night...
(*CT* 470; trans. Faulkner, 2007)

Pakhet appears to have had a New Kingdom cult dedicated to her in *Beni Hassan,* in Middle Egypt, where a rock-cut sanctuary was located. Also, in this area, Pakhet possessed a cemetery housing sacred cats that had been sacrificed to her (Wilkinson, 2003, p. 180). Ancient Egypt had a rather lucrative business in the realm of mummified animal votives. Though we may assume they loved cats (and some evidence suggests they did) they were not squeamish about sacrificing them to Netjerut such as Pakhet and Bastet (with the exception of one's that appear to have been kept as beloved pets; Ikram, 2003, p. 91).

The connection between lionesses and cats, and the Eye of Ra, is evident through the clear relationship between Bastet and Sekhmet. Mafdet is another feline Netjeret with protective qualities. Cats were considered useful in ancient Egypt because of their ability to hunt rodents, snakes, and scorpions. As a hunter of snakes, and a feline, this led them to be associated with the Eye of Ra who protected the creator from the chaos serpent (*PT* 438). One rather interesting spell invokes Mafdet's protection and involves reciting a text over a loaf of bread in the form of a phallus inscribed with the names of one's enemies, which is wrapped in fatty meat and fed to a cat; in an act of sympathetic magic it was believed that Mafdet would consume the enemies just as the cat consumed the bread (Pinch, 2006, p. 88).

Shesmetet is a very ancient name which often appears in association with Sekhmet and Bastet. She may have been an independent Netjeret from Nubia, as well as a form of Sekhmet or Bastet (Wilkinson, 2003, p. 183). Unfortunately references to her are scarce, though her appearance in the *PT* places her in a funerary context giving birth to and/or mothering the reborn Pharaoh (*PT* 248; Wilkinson, 2003, p. 183). At the temple of *El Kab,* south of Luxor, several Eye Netjerut were equated with the local Netjeret Nekhbet, who took the form of a vulture. On one temple relief there, the Wandering Eye myth is recorded and depicts Hut-hor as the left lunar Eye, and Nekhbet as the right solar Eye (Richter, 2010, pp. 162, 166). Nekhbet was also paired with the cobra Netjeret Wadjet, who together were referred to as the Two Ladies who protected Upper and Lower Egypt respectively (Pinch, 2002, pp. 211-213). Nekhbet's vulture often appears beside Wadjet's cobra – the uraeus – on the Pharaoh's brow. Egyptian queens often wore vulture headdresses in identification with the protective Eye's, Nekhbet and Mut.

There are many other Netjerut who bore the epithet, Eye of Ra. The ones listed above are some of the most common. The Eye of Ra was the Eye of the creator himself looking down upon creation through the solar disc. This sun disc, this Eye, was Ra's daughter whose protection extended beyond Ra and his earthly heirs (Egypt's Pharaohs), protecting those she gazed upon, or annihilating those who threatened creation or displeased her. Rituals and festivals involving the Eye of Ra demonstrate this balance, by invoking her healing powers and celebrating her return, as well as working to ease her anger and invoke her protection, both earthly and mythical. The Eyes of Ra could be invoked together as well as on their own as is evident from a discovery of four clay lionesses which were positioned surrounding the image of the Netjer Wesir, who represented the deceased Pharaoh; these lionesses have been identified as Sekhmet, Wadjet, Bastet, and Shesmetet, all Eyes of Ra. Their positioning suggests that the Pharaoh/Wesir was protected from all four directions (Raven, 2012, p. 117).

Syncretism

In ancient Egyptian religion it was possible for multiple contradictory things to be true synonymously. One Netjeret could be named the Mother of all Netjeru and within the same text a different Netjeret holds the same title. The Egyptians believed in a concept now known as syncretism, which meant that Netjeru could merge with one another taking on the attributes of the Netjer they merged with. It was possible for the merged form, affectively a deity in its own right, to exist at the same time as the independent forms it was comprised of (Hornung, 1996, p. 91); for example, Sekhmet and Bastet merged to form a new Netjeret – Sekhmet-Bastet – containing the attributes of each, and who then went on to exist independently. It is also important to remember that when we talk about ancient Egyptian religion today, we are trying to include an extensive period of time, and numerous cults from settlements along the Nile, comprising those sanctioned by the state and those practiced by the common people; therefore, many variations of beliefs, mythologies, and Netjeru can be identified.

A Contemporary Pagan Perspective

Considering how many Eyes of Ra there are and how many appear identical in reliefs, it may be of use for modern devotees to become familiar with the traditional hieroglyphic orthography of Sekhmet's name. Often depictions of the Netjeru and people appear with labels close by (or embedded within an accompanying text). By learning the typical ways that names are spelt, one may look upon reliefs and identify where references to the Netjeru are being made, as well as identify which Netjer is represented. Familiarity with such spellings is also useful for if one wishes to inscribe offerings or use the name instead of an icon on an altar or shrine (fig. 3). There may be variations in spelling in reliefs but identifying common signs will often be clear enough.

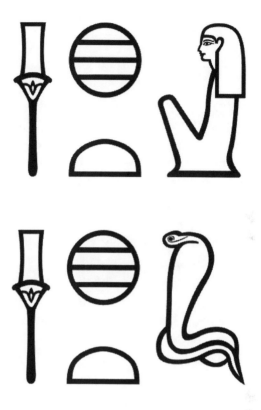

Figure 3. Orthography of Sekhmet's name in hieroglyphs

When revering Sekhmet today, one may find it fulfilling to explore the various other Eyes of Ra and how they may provide new insights regarding this role. Though some Eyes of Ra may merge with Sekhmet, others maintain a distinct identity and may complement one another in rituals, festivals, and upon altars. The combination of Hut-hor, Bastet, and Sekhmet are a good example of this.

The Eyes of Ra are powerful Netjerut and symbols for contemporary Pagans to invoke today when seeking protection. The chaos serpent can be interpreted as a metaphor for various destructive forces (such as diseases), behaviours (such as deforestation and pollution), and in some cases specific groups of people, who pose a very real risk to the environment, to society, marginalised communities, and so on. Sekhmet's protection is something that contemporary people can still pray for, whether one is serving in the military, working on a crisis ward, supporting victims of abuse, or attending social justice protests. There are numerous reasons why someone may seek her protection today. Some may choose to conduct rituals against the metaphorical, or real, chaos serpent, though they should take care and ensure that Sekhmet is on their side first! The ancient Egyptians understood and respected Sekhmet's power, including her anger and her ability to direct this anger towards one's enemies, or indeed towards oneself. We may be less superstitious today, but knowing that Sekhmet is a Netjeret historically associated with destruction, plague, and unfriendly daemonic entities, it is wise to approach her with respect. This does not mean I advocate a fearful approach, as many of her contemporary devotees praise her healing and comforting presence; however, such devotees maintain a level of respect for her less benevolent face nonetheless (Lucid & Pontiac, 2018). As with any powerful natural force, awareness and respect is wise.

Chapter 5

Temples & Cults

Despite Sekhmet's widespread influence, countless iconographic representations, and appearances in ritual texts, there are very few, if any, sites today that survive dedicated to her specifically. Sekhmet's cult centre was located at Memphis, close to modern day Cairo, although this location has yet to yield substantial archaeological remains of her temple there. Instead, Sekhmet can be found in various syncretised forms with other Netjerut across Egypt, appearing in temples dedicated to Mut, Bastet, and Hut-hor. As mentioned in a previous chapter, the temple ritual offering of sacrificed animal blood involved invoking Sekhmet, regardless of who would ultimately receive the offering. Amulets depicting lioness Netjerut and magico-medical spells invoking her name are widespread. Thus, the lack of an official "temple of Sekhmet" is by no means indicative of a lack of reverence.

Egyptian Temples & Sites

Karnak Temple Complex
One of the most famous locations of Sekhmet's cult known to contemporary Pagans is not actually a temple dedicated to Sekhmet. The Temple of Amun, within the Karnak complex in modern Luxor, covers a substantial area with an extensive history of building, rebuilding, and modifications. Located towards the northern part of the main temple is a smaller one dedicated to Ptah, Sekhmet's consort. Ptah's temple dates to at least the 17th dynasty approximately 1580 BCE and underwent numerous changes during the Kushite and Ptolemaic dynasties (the Kushite Dynasty – the 25th Dynasty - was when Egypt was under Kushite/Nubian rule; Thiers, 2011, pp. 20-21; Wilkinson,

2000, p. 163). Much of the temple's ruins are open air and accessible; however, the sanctuaries at the rear of the temple are still protected by a roof and are usually locked. Access to these sanctuaries may be granted by tour guides, or by informal requests (along with *baksheesh,* or tips) made to temple guards. There are three chapels contained within this area, one dedicated to Ptah, one to Nefertem, and one to Hut-hor (Wilkinson, 2000, p. 163).

Upon entering Hut-hor's small, dark enclosure one will instantly meet the famous black statue of Sekhmet, illuminated by a shaft of light from a modern opening in the ceiling (fig. 4). This statue likely originated from the Mut precinct, also within the Karnak complex, but somehow made its way to Hut-hor's chapel. Considering the mythological connection between these Netjerut, and Sekhmet's role as Ptah's consort, it does not feel inappropriate for her statue to now reside here; however, I feel it is important to honour Hut-hor here too, as it was originally a sacred space dedicated to her. There are many stories from modern pilgrims describing their experiences within this chapel, face-to-face with Sekhmet. There are so few inner sanctuaries of Egyptian temples that contain (intact) statues of Netjeru, that this chapel feels significant. The contrast between the enclosure's sealed darkness and the shaft of sunlight upon Sekhmet's leonine face, emphasises a feeling of 'otherness' and sacredness. Standing in a room containing only yourself (and fellow pilgrims) and Sekhmet's statue emphasises a feeling of intimacy, of meeting the Netjeret and bridging the gap between the truly ancient and the very present.

Figure 4. Statue of Sekhmet now located in the Temple of Ptah, Karnak (author's own photo)

Within the Karnak complex is the temple of Amun's consort, Mut. Mut's precinct was linked to the main Temple of Amun by a processional route, once lined with hundreds of seated and standing black granite statues of Sekhmet, famously erected by the Pharaoh, Amenhotep III (Wilkinson, 2000, pp. 55, 163). Within this temple precinct Sekhmet is pictured in a relief, receiving offerings of music alongside Mut, as well as some of the large statues still standing *in situ* (Capel & Markoe, 1997, p.

136). It was within Mut's precinct that annual festivals relating to the appeasement of Sekhmet were conducted.

Statues of Sekhmet

Most of the famous seated statues of Sekhmet can be dated to the reign of Amenhotep III, with some of the standing ones likely belonging to a later date. The exact number of Sekhmet statues in these variations remains inconclusive though appear to total up to 1000 (and counting). Obtaining an accurate number is complicated by their now scattered status in museums across the world. Outside of Karnak the statues have been unearthed during recent excavations at *Kom el-Hettan*, Amenhotep III's mortuary temple, located near to Luxor (Toonen *et al.*, 2019, p. 202), as well as the temple of Sekhmet- Hut-hor in the Delta site of *Kom el-Hisn* (Wilkinson, 2000, p. 108). One hypothesis for why there are so many of these statues is that they form a kind of stone calendar with two statues for everyday of the year, intended to protect Egypt from plague each day (Pinch, 2006, p. 143); however, this now appears unlikely as hundreds more have been discovered since the original estimate of 730 (Bryan, 2020).

Another intriguing feature of these statues was shared by Hourig Sourouzian during a conference held in Luxor in 2016. Sourouzian described her discovery that a number of the Sekhmet statues had once been decorated with red paint, notably around the eyes (Sourouzian *et al.* 2016). This is a powerful thing to consider, conjuring up images of what these statues may have looked like as the Eye of Ra peering down upon human viewers with her fiery red gaze.

Abusir

The earliest sanctuary potentially dedicated to Sekhmet was located in the mortuary temple belonging to the Pharaoh Sahure, who lived during the Old Kingdom's 5th Dynasty. Sahure's pyramid and mortuary temple are located at Abusir, in northern Egypt (Wilkinson, 2003, p. 182). Sahure continued to receive a funerary cult up until the end of the Ptolemaic period, nearly 2500 years after his death (Smoláriková, 2002)! During the New Kingdom Sahure's cult transformed into the cult of 'Sekhmet of Sahure', whereupon the deceased Pharaoh took the form of Sekhmet (Gaber, 2003, p. 18). This is attestable through literary documentation, and though a temple no longer stands today, it is known that the walls included many reliefs of Bastet (Germond, 1981, p. 343). Within the pyramid of Sahure, an Old Kingdom scene was later adapted to accommodate the cult of Sekhmet. The scene depicts the King offering wine to Sekhmet stating:

> *Wine and libation for the ka of the mistress of the two lands, Sekhmet of Sahure.*
> (Poo, 2009, p. 39).

Outside of Abusir there is evidence that this particular cult also practiced at the New Kingdom village of *Deir el-Medina*, with festivals related to it observed during the season of *peret* (Gaber, 2003, pp. 19, 28).

Bubastis

The temple of Bastet at Bubastis, modern *Tell-Basta,* is well-attested in the historical records; what remains today, however, is scattered ruins and severed pillars, resting in such a pattern that the architectural plan can still be traced (Wilkinson, 2000, pp. 109-110). The site has experienced illicit digging and plundering in the past with much of its information unfortunately stolen or damaged. Nevertheless, we know that Bubastis was a significant cult centre for Bastet and according to Herodotus, enjoyed large festival gatherings (Herodotus, *Book 2*, 60). Although dedicated to Bastet, it is very likely that Sekhmet would have been a part of the festivities in some way and appeared in certain locations of the temple.

Kom el-Hisn

Aforementioned were the statues of Sekhmet unearthed at *Kom el-Hisn*. This was the site of a temple of Hut-hor-Sekhmet, dating to the reign of Senwosret I in the Middle Kingdom's 12th dynasty, where both Hut-hor and Sekhmet were known as 'Mistress of *Imu*', after the site's ancient name (Sakr, 2005, p. 353). Sadly, much of the temple has not survived today, with only the floorplan remaining detectable.

A Contemporary Pagan Perspective

In my experience, Karnak's temple of Ptah, and its Hut-hor chapel is one of the few places in modern Egypt where tourists/pilgrims are welcome to enter with outward spiritual intent. Many other locations forbid overt spiritual practices or suspected acts of 'meditation', which I have come to understand in this context includes reflective stillness. Though this is disappointing to many, we must respect the religious landscape of modern Egypt. The guards in Karnak, however, appear to be aware of how popular Hut-hor's chapel is to tourists who are more than happy to offer *baksheesh* in exchange for the opportunity to stand in the chapel privately for five minutes. This offers people, such as myself, the chance to kneel before a statue of Sekhmet in prayer and within an ancient Egyptian sacred space; nowhere else have I been able to do this, certainly not with any privacy. For that I am very grateful to this temple's modern guardians. Though many modern pilgrims visit the Karnak chapel to meet Sekhmet, and commonly refer to it as 'Sekhmet's temple', I think there is great wisdom to be learned in recognising its original dedication to Hut-hor, and how the two Netjerut share the space today.

Contemporary pagans in significant numbers have reported spiritual interactions with statues of Sekhmet from numerous museums around the world. Many are familiar for example, with the collection on display in London's British Museum, which often receive considerable attention from spiritually-inclined visitors. Down in the storerooms I have had the pleasure of viewing several more of these exquisite sculptures. It is abundantly clear that these statues of Sekhmet actively communicate with people thousands of years after their creation and hundreds, if not thousands, of miles away from their original context. Many modern devotees consider the statues to be 'living' and imbued with Sekhmet's presence, or her *ka*. It is not necessary to enter a temple dedicated to Sekhmet, though that would be amazing, as one glance at her sculpted face can be sufficient to occupy the surrounding area as her sacred space. This can be achieved through even the smallest of statues, figurines, and representations, which is not at all surprising considering her name means 'incarnate power'. The evidence of this is abundantly clear through these experiences provoked by her image alone. Many devotees have reported experiencing statues of Sekhmet animating, giving off heat, communicating with them, and in some cases compelling them to bow or kneel. Hank Wesselman describes the statues as a 'doorway through which she can access this physical world and through which we can access the transpersonal worlds in expanded state of awareness' (Wesselman, 2011, 109). Such reports confirm that Sekhmet is indeed active in the world today, with something to say to devotees who visit her statues in museums.

Visiting Sekhmet's statue within Hut-hor's Karnak shrine was a life-changing experience for a woman named Genevieve Vaughan. Her well-known story recalls a trip to Egypt which included visiting Sekhmet's statue. Despite having little prior knowledge of Sekhmet, Genevieve was moved to pray to the Netjeret, asking her to bless her with a child, which she had been trying to conceive for some time; in exchange, Sekhmet was promised a modern temple dedicated to her. Sekhmet agreed to this deal and Genevieve became a mother of three daughters over the course of ten years. This is the origin story for the Temple of Goddess Spirituality dedicated to Sekhmet in the Nevada Desert, USA, built in 1993 (Key, 2011a, p. 3). At a time when few contemporary Pagan and Goddess temples exist compared to the ancient world, temples such as this are significant. Sekhmet is able to reach her devotees today through her living statues, both ancient and modern, through 2D and 3D images, and her symbols. This is a Netjeret who can be felt through the sunlight or the flame of a candle. Temples are valuable spaces to honour her, but as in the ancient past, Sekhmet's presence permeates the natural world.

Chapter 6

Rituals & Festivals

As previously mentioned, Sekhmet was a Netjeret who governed matters in life that posed very real threats to the Egyptian people as well as offered literally life-saving help. She therefore was regularly and annually appeased by the people and her doctor-priests. Considering the wide expanse of time and distances across Egypt it is likely that her rituals had many variations according to local needs; however, the temple priesthood were traditionalists and had common ways of doing things. Each priest, priestess, musician, and chantress had their own role to play, with a special few allowed into the inner sanctuary of the Netjer/et. *Wab* priests, or 'pure' priests, maintained a sufficient level of cleanliness, especially prior to entering the temple and were considered pure enough to stand in the presence of the divine (Teeter, 2011, p. 20). There were also liturgical priests who were trained to recite the extensive ritual texts that are recorded in temple religious practice, as well as various musicians and dancers employed to entertain the Netjeru.

The focus of rituals dedicated to Sekhmet were an effort to keep her appeased so that she would not use her great power for destructive purposes. Sometimes this approach is framed in such a way by modern scholars that it suggests her priests aimed to keep her 'sedated by a constant flow of adoration, and... drunken ritual' (Aziz, 2018, p. 35); however, a dear friend of mine pointed out to me that this rings of arguably sexist overtones, suggesting that Sekhmet's feminine rage needed to be pacified through intoxication. In other words, it suggests that to keep Sekhmet under control, and her anger suppressed, she was regularly drugged. It evokes an image of a dominant ruler keeping the lioness in captivity, keeping Sekhmet on a leash, tamed and passive until it suits him to release her upon his enemies. This is not something I find to be consistent with the fact that she nevertheless managed to ravage the land prior to, and during the inundation. Attempts to contain her power seemed futile. Instead, one would be better advised to seek to *appease* the Mighty One than to control or pacify her power. In addition to rituals of appeasement, the Egyptians held festivals in celebration of Sekhmet and Hut-hor which were occasions of great joy.

Offerings

Whether or not she had temples dedicated exclusively to her, Sekhmet would have received cult offerings alongside those she shared sacred spaces with. The standard temple offering formulae was spoken by a priest on behalf of the Pharaoh and often consisted of offering incense, bread, beer, and sacrificed meat such as poultry. Numerous temple reliefs depict royalty and priests approaching the Netjeru wafting incense, presenting tables of food, and even holding special symbols such as the *ankh* to their noses, offering the breath of life. Keeping Sekhmet well-fed, libated, and entertained with music was an essential part of her ancient cult. A ritual like this is depicted upon the walls of the temple of Mut, where a female temple musician plays a harp, behind the king who shakes two sistra before the images of Mut seated and Sekhmet standing behind her (Capel & Markoe, 1997, p. 135, fig. 8). The musician sings:

I am the perfect sistrum player for the Golden Lady, who pacifies* the heart of my mistress every day.
(Capel & Markoe, 1997, p. 136; *I would suggest 'who *pleases* the heart' here)

We know that common people made use of protective amulets, spells, and prayers invoking Sekhmet's protection, or warding against her wrath. It is likely that they would have also made offerings to appease her, though less formalised than the temple cults.

Rituals & Festivals

The Appeasement of Sekhmet, sḥtp sḥmt
The ancient Egyptian New Year, *wep ronpet*, took place between July and August with the heliacal rise of the star Sopdet (Greek Sirius) coinciding with the coming of the inundation. Awaiting the flood was a time of great vulnerability, occupying a liminal space between the old year and the new. It was possible for many malevolent forces to take advantage, and the risk of plague and destruction was high when the flood finally arrived. Festive observances for the New Year would have varied across time and across Egypt. One way was to exchange amuletic gifts with other people for protection; numerous amulets of cats, lionesses, and associated Netjeret were popular, for example. Spells could also be bought from magician-priests, such as one entitled, 'The Book of the Last Day of the Year', which was recited over a piece of cloth and worn around a person's neck to ward off harm (Borghouts, 1978, pp. 12-14, no. 13).

The Pharaoh and priests of Sekhmet also responded to these risks in formal temple rituals such as the *sehetep Sekhmet,* the 'appeasement of Sekhmet' (Wilkinson, 2003, p. 182). It is significant to note that in the context of these rituals, the word *sḥtp* is sometimes translated as 'pacification'. Whether one chooses to translate this word as 'appeasement' or 'pacification' determines the interpretive approach one has to Sekhmet. As suggested above, the latter perpetuates an idea of exercising control over Sekhmet's anger; the former indicates a level of respect, hoping that she will look favourably upon the propitiator. One interesting practice from the Late Period involved the Pharaoh applying an ointment from a *bꜣs*-jar (named after the Netjeret

Bastet) to protect him from the Eye Netjeret's wrath at the New Year (Amgad, 2018, p. 36).

These appeasement rituals could involve reciting the *Litanies of Sekhmet* which are recorded across numerous temples. These involved reciting Sekhmet's epithets and asking her to protect the Pharaoh (and his land). Rituals to appease Sekhmet occurred at various intervals throughout the year, to ensure that Sekhmet would offer her protection. Jean Yoyette hypothesised that the commission of hundreds of Sekhmet statues by Amenhotep III were used for this ritual, noticing how the epithets inscribed upon the statues corresponded to those contained within the litanies. Writing in the 1980's Yoyette had estimated that the statues numbered 730, leading to the suggestion that there were two statues for each day of the year (Yoyette, 1980, p. 64). As the litanies clearly beseeched Sekhmet to protect the Pharaoh and the land from the annual threat of pestilence, these statues could act as dual guardians for each day. However as indicated in the previous chapter, the number of 730 was an earlier estimate and more recently hundreds more have been found (Bryan, 1997, p. 60; Bryan, 2020).

Betsy Bryan believes that the numerous Sekhmet statues found in the mortuary temple of Amenhotep III instead relate to the *Sed* festival, which occurred every 30 years of a Pharaoh's reign. This might explain why so many statues were created, for this was a significant occasion, where Sekhmet would ensure the Pharaoh's enduring health and success; it also would have taken years to plan for, as would the sculpting of hundreds of statues (Bryan, 1997, p. 60; Bryan, 2020). These were certainly part of a long-term planned project. Amenhotep III's *Sed* festival appears to have coincided with an annual appeasement of Sekhmet ritual around the final two days of the second month in the season of *peret*; these were days considered to be unlucky due to their closeness to the winter solstice when the sun was at its weakest (Bryan, 1997, pp. 61, 66).

Sekhmet and various other Eye Neterjut could all be appeased through various methods, including anointing one's person from a *bⁱs*-jar, reciting specific prayers and litanies, offering wine or beer, shaking sistra, and wearing special amulets (Amgad, 2018, p. 40).

The Overthrowing of 'Apep

The *BRP* contains *The Book of Overthrowing 'Apep*, which involves numerous spells to defeat the chaos serpent, who represented cosmic chaos as well as the earthly enemies of the Pharaoh and state. This was a serious ritual conducted within the temples, performed by priests in locations such as at Mut's Karnak temple; it would have involved sympathetic magic and the recitation of spells by lector priests (Pinch, 2006, pp. 86-87). As well as invoking powerful Netjerut, such as Sekhmet, the priests would have recited the true names of 'Apep, which was a magical technique to take command over him. His names could be written on papyrus and burned, sealed inside a box, or buried (Pinch, 2006, p. 87).

This ritual reflects a type of magic known as execration texts and aimed to actively attack threats and enemies (Ritner, 2008, pp. 137-139). *The Overthrowing of 'Apep* was more serious than others, as it was typically concerned with cosmic threats to creation, rather than more direct kinds of danger, such as human 'rebels', those using harmful magic, and the angry spirits of the dead (Ritner, 2008, pp. 139-141). As Sekhmet is one of the principle defenders of Ra, and therefore his creations, such rituals can be considered a regular part of her cult, even though the intention is not directly to worship her.

The Festivals of Drunkenness and the Beautiful Feast of the Valley

There are two main feasts known as drunkenness festivals which are recorded in the temple of Mut at Karnak (Bryan, 2017, 2020).

One took place at the beginning of the year and another towards the end, which was known as the Beautiful Feast of the Valley during the New Kingdom.

The drunkenness festival at the start of the year involved drinking in joyous celebration of the Wandering Eye's return, taking place on a full moon. There are several dates recorded for this latter festival, such as the first month of the year (Jensen, 2017, p. 297) and the winter months of *Tybi* and *Mechir* (their Greek names). At midwinter, the Egyptians observed that the sun then started moving northwards again, thus mirroring the return of the Wandering Eye (Richter, 2010, pp. 160, 169).

The festival's primary congregation would have consisted of members of the elite, who gathered at the 'place of drunkenness', a courtyard within Mut's temple precinct. A description of this festival appears upon the temple walls, known as the *Medamûd Hymn*, and appears to reference the celebration of the Wandering Eye's return, owing to its joyful tone. The hymn describes how the festivities began at dusk, when the lamps were lit for the evening:

> *Come, oh Golden One, who eats of praise,*
> *because the food of her desire is dancing,*
> *who shines on the festival at the time of lighting (the lamps),*
> *who is content with the dancing at night.*
> *Come! the procession is in the place of inebriation,*
> *that hall of travelling through the marshes.*
> *Its performance is set,*
> *its order is in effect,*
> *without anything lacking in it.*
> (*The Medamûd Hymn*; trans. Darnell, 1995, pp. 49-50)

Not only were participants consuming alcohol, but they were also partaking of other mind-altering substances. One indicator of this is shown by the addition of a lotus blossom hieroglyph as a determinative for the word 'drunkenness' in the above hymn. The Egyptian lotus, *nymphaea lotus*, is known to have narcotic qualities. Additionally, numerous scenes depicting the festival involve celebrants drinking from vessels in the shape of lotus flowers (Bryan, 2020). Celebrants would drink this mixture to the point of losing consciousness (Jensen, 2017, p. 297). Once they had fallen asleep, temple musicians would re-awaken them with the sound of percussion instruments and lead them to gather in front of the Netjeret's icon; here they would experience *maa* – a mutual 'seeing', where the celebrants looked upon the Netjeret, and she gazed back at them (Bryan, 2017). Thus, the reason for intoxication had a firmly sacred purpose: to ensure celebrants were receptive to divine epiphany.

The Beautiful Feast of the Valley was a festival specific to the city of *waset,* in modern Luxor. It would have taken place towards the end of the year during summer, on a new moon before the flood, when the sun was intense and the land longing for water (Teeter, 2011, p. 67). Participants would have consumed concoctions of a red alcoholic beverage, seeking to appease Sekhmet, in reference to the Myth of the Destruction of Mankind. Celebrants would have travelled across the river to the west bank mortuary temple of Hatshepsut, in *Deir el-Bahri*. They would celebrate within the temple precinct (though not within the inner sanctuary), before departing for their families' tombs to receive a divine epiphany of the Netjeret and commune with their ancestors. Access to the temple and substantial tombs would have been a privilege belonging to the elite, though common people might have had a humble variation. The goddess usually named during the epiphany is Hut-hor, the beneficent side of Sekhmet (Bryan, 2020).

Records of drunkenness festivals and associated rituals appear in over twenty temples from the Ptolemaic period, suggesting its widespread popularity and potential for variation. They describe festivities involving processions, singing, feasting, and sailing sacred barques on temple lakes (Richter, 2010, p. 155). According to Richter, these descriptions not only serve as records of their happening, but are an integrated part of the ritual performances themselves, for they appear on areas of the temples where these events may have taken place. This is suggested from a temple in *Wadi el-Hallel* (near modern Luxor) and Hut-hor's temple at Dendera (Richter, 2010, p. 155).

In her discussion of one festival of Drunkenness in Dendera, René Preys identifies a ritual of 'making an *isheru* lake', an artificial crescent-shaped lake found in several temple complexes, including that of Bastet at Bubastis (Preys, 1999, pp. 263, 266-267). During the festival these lakes represented the location of the Wandering Eye's return, where she drank of the waters, and where she bathed. Records from Dendera describe a fascinating ritual involving sixteen vases, filled with flood water and poured into an *isheru* – or crescent-shaped – basin around the feet of the Netjeret's statue (Preys, 1999, p. 263). Whilst Preys asserts that this ritual occurred within the walls of the temple, Richter offers an alternative suggestion that the ritual took place on the lake itself, with the icon of the Netjeret sailing upon the water as she brings the inundation with her (Richter, 2010, p. 174). As this particular ritual was located in Dendera, the icon is most likely to have belonged to Hut-hor; however, according to the myth, Sekhmet emerged from Hut-hor's rage and therefore, her return to the beneficent image of Hut-hor for this festival is understandable.

CT 890 mentions a festival involving on "who sought her who is far away on the day of the festival of red linen..." This references the distant, wandering Netjeret in association with red linen. As one of Sekhmet's epithets is 'Lady of the Red Linen' this spell appears to refer to a festival involving her, though at an earlier date than those mentioned above (Richter, 2010, pp. 158-159).

The Festival of Bastet

Although Bubastis was the cult centre of Bastet, Sekhmet was certainly present in some way, due to their strong connection as Eyes of Ra. A festival dedicated to Bastet was vividly captured by the Greek historian Herodotus after his visit to Egypt:

> When the people are on their way to Bubastis, they go by river, a great number in every boat, men and women together. Some of the women make a noise with rattles, others play flutes all the way, while the rest of the women, and the men, sing and clap their hands. As they travel by river to Bubastis, whenever they come near any other town they bring their boat near the bank; then some of the women do as I have said, while some shout mockery of the women of the town; others dance, and others stand up and lift their skirts. They do this whenever they come alongside any riverside town. But when they have reached Bubastis, they make a festival with great sacrifices, and more wine is drunk at this feast than in the whole year besides. It is customary for men and women (but not children) to assemble there to the number of seven hundred thousand, as the people of the place say.
>
> (Herodotus, Book 2, 60; trans. Godley, 1920)

This festival is distinct from the Festival of Drunkenness in honour of the Wandering Eye; however, owing to its similar theme and connection to a feline Eye Netjeret, this festival could be appreciated by devotees of Sekhmet also.

These festivals of drunkenness and of Bastet demonstrate how Sekhmet's cults certainly had a jovial side to them. They were not all preoccupied with medicine, protection, and defence. Sekhmet and Hut-hor are intimately connected through their mythology and so just as Sekhmet can be understood as Hut-Hor's aggressive counterpart, Hut-hor is Sekhmet's benevolent side. Sekhmet's mythical affinity with beer and lotuses indicate her role as a Netjeret of sacred drunkenness. When she is not defending the Creator and spreading pestilence, Sekhmet shines her life-giving sunlight upon the land, revelling in her devotee's musical sistrum playing, overseeing festive love-making, and partaking in alcoholic offerings.

A Contemporary Pagan Perspective

As Sekhmet emerged from Hut-hor's unleashed power and fury, provoked through those threatening creation and life, she can be ritually invoked in times of great need. One might find suitable purpose for execration rituals, or summoning Sekhmet's defensive power, though I advise responsible caution in doing so. Other rituals to Sekhmet sought to encourage her favour and blessing. As such, for a more common practice one could easily adapt the standard offering formula according to the offerings you may wish to provide. Below is such a formula, with the approximated pronunciation above, the English translation below, and suggested offerings. I have only provided offerings that the Egyptians would have had words for and used, but you can of course insert whatever you feel is suitable. This formula is more accurately a 'voice offering', which means it is designed to be spoken aloud; furthermore, by saying it, it becomes true, and so you do not actually have to offer the physical versions of everything you state – though you can do so if you like.

I have also inserted Sekhmet's name and three epithets here and replaced the word for Pharaoh (*nisu*) with the word for follower (*shemsu*). Though the ancient priests would have made offerings on behalf of the Pharaoh it may not be relevant for all contemporary Pagans today (with the exception of some Kemetic groups who follow a modern *nisu*):

hotep di shemsu Sekhmet, nebet-neby, iret net Ra, nebet Ankh-Tawy
An offering which the follower gives (to) Sekhmet, Mistress of Flame, Eye of Ra, Lady of Ankh-Tawy
di-ef / di-es peret-kheru ___, ___, ___

So that he / she may give a voice offering (of) ___, ___, ___
[offerings]
nebet neferet wabet ankeht netjeret eem
Everything good and pure on which a Goddess lives...
The Egyptian version also includes a line for offering to the *ka*
of the deceased/ancestors, which you may also include:
En ka hen eemakhoo ___.
For the *ka* of the revered one ___ [name].

Suggested offering translations:

akhet = flame
dua = praise
et = bread
henkhet = beer
hetpet = offerings
hesi = to sing/make music
irep = wine
merhet = oil
moo = water
senetjer = incense

Contemporary offerings made to Sekhmet may comprise of the above, as well as red ales, beer, wine, spices such as cinnamon and chilli, and anything that reminds one of fire, heat, and the sun. Offering raw, or cooked meat is also an option for some devotees today. If one wishes to avoid alcohol, then red fruit juice can be offered, or water can be coloured by ochre or food colouring. Alternatively, one might be seeking to appeal to Sekhmet's calmer aspects, and therefore may wish to cool off the Netjeret's heat by pouring cold, clean water and by wafting incense. Shaking a percussion instrument such as a rattle, singing, dancing, and reciting prayers are also all things that could be offered to Sekhmet today.

In terms of festivals in honour of Sekhmet, those described above were deeply imbedded within the cycles and observances made of the ancient Egyptian landscape. As many modern devotees of Sekhmet do not live in Egypt, and considering that the Nile no longer floods, contemporary Pagans need to reconsider Sekhmet's mythology for their own context (without forgetting the original). Choosing when to observe modern variations of the festivals remains extremely subjective and dependant on the individual devotee's location, needs, and interpretations. Some may follow an ancient Egyptian calendar applied to modern dates. Others may take a wholly modern approach. Whatever the choice, one should keep in mind the primary themes of Sekhmet's festivals, that being the Eye's withdrawal and return, and her appeasement.

Summer Solstice – Pleasing the Eye

Today, as in antiquity, the summer solstice remains an appropriate time for the Appeasement of Sekhmet. At this time of the year the days are at their longest and it is usually the warmest part of the year (though defining 'warm' depends on one's location). Depending on where one lives, the appeal for Sekhmet to avert her angry gaze at midsummer may indeed be necessary, such as in areas that suffer summer droughts. Those who experience milder climates may find other significance in Sekhmet's mythology related to the Destruction of Mankind, such as advocating for environmental protection.

Beautiful Feast of the Valley

As well as revering Sekhmet, one may wish to honour her counterpart, Hut-hor, and therefore recreate an interpretation of the Beautiful Feast of the Valley. Traditionally this would have occurred during the summer and would have involved visiting and feasting with the beloved dead and the ancestors. Some cultures today honour their ancestors in the autumn or winter, rather than in the summer, so placement of this festival is up to your intuition.

Winter Solstice – The Return of the Wandering Eye

Following the winter solstice, the sun appears to move northward and after six months of increasingly short days, the days begin to grow longer and the sun grows in strength. This can be a sign of the return of the Wandering Eye and a cause for great celebration, where feasts can be shared and fires lit. One might choose to place another Festival of Drunkenness here. If drinking alcohol features, please do so responsibly and keep in mind the sacred intention for this. In ancient Egypt these festivals were not an excuse for drunken indulgence. Though consuming alcohol encouraged merriment, its purpose was to shift one's consciousness so that they might better witness and communicate with the divine.

Recreating rituals such as those conducted during the Festivals of Drunkenness is entirely possible today with some creative license. This would involve feasting and drinking – though alcohol consumption is not strictly necessary, especially for those who choose to abstain from this. In fact, Betsy Bryan has suggested that not all celebrants indulged in this aspect (Bryan, 2020). The purpose of drinking in this context was a strictly sacred one, intended to shift one's consciousness. There are many ways that one can achieve an altered state of consciousness and so it is important to choose an appropriate method for yourself. After indulging in the gifts of Hut-hor for the evening, one may then attempt to sleep for a few hours and arrange to be woken at a certain time (ideally by music). This groggy awakening could be followed by standing or sitting before the Netjeret's icon, inviting divine communication and (hopefully) a mutual 'seeing', or divine epiphany.

The rituals pertaining to the Appeasement of Sekhmet can

occur annually, or at regular intervals throughout the year. They could involve reciting translations of the *Litanies of Sekhmet* (Chapter 7), shaking sistra, and making offerings of beer. Likewise, the return of the Wandering Eye can be observed through pouring libations into a crescent-shaped bowl before her icon, or through sending a miniature vessel – such as a paper boat – out onto a body of water.

In whatever way one approaches a modern interpretation of the mythic cycle and recreating festivals, I believe it is important to remember their original context and to appreciate the journey that has occurred to reach modern manifestations. Therefore, the original myths can be retold, in the context of the ancient Egyptian landscape and how this affected the Egyptian people, whilst also bringing the stories into the modern day, and how Sekhmet continues to affect people both within and beyond Egypt today. This acknowledges the rich heritage that has been inherited and shared across cultures and time.

Chapter 7

Magic & Prayers

Ancient Egyptian Magic

The ancient Egyptians recognised an energetic force which permeated all things to varying degrees, known as *heka*. This force, sometimes personified as a Netjer, was a current which could be tapped in to create changes in the world and is sometimes likened to 'magic'. According to a text addressed to the Pharaoh Merikare, *heka* was created as a method 'to ward off the blow of events' (Lichtheim, 1973, p. 106). It was considered a part of the natural world, rather than something supernatural and could be practiced by people both literate and illiterate, professionally and vocationally (Ritner, 2008, p. 8; Raven, 2012, p. 29). Sekhmet's role in healing kept her in close contact with the magical practices of her magician-priests. Spells involving Sekhmet most often involved deliberate appeals for her protection (prevention) or healing (resolution), and were accompanied by ritual action, either in the form of sympathetic magic, or the application of medicinal treatments. Such spells often take a bipartite or tripartite form, containing an explanation or rubric, followed by actions to be done and words to be said (Pinch, 2003, p. 68). Even liturgical prayers possessed a magical quality, where through praising the Netjeret it was also hoped that she would be appeased and inclined to offer beneficent support; such prayers would have been accompanied by ritual action, and could be recited during festivals.

Symbols of Sekhmet

To the ancient Egyptians words possessed great power and what was said or written could become reality (Pinch, 2006, pp. 18-19). To write, read, or speak Sekhmet's name was to invite its meaning, summoning incarnate '(female) power'. For this reason, the hieroglyphic orthography of her name could be used as a symbol to represent her (shared in Chapter 4). Her name is often written with the triliteral hieroglyph representing the word, *sḫm* in the form of a sistrum rattle. There were two types of sistrum rattles, one formed by a loop of metal and threaded with bars and chimes, named a *sesheshet*. The other was the naos-shrine shaped sistrum, named a *sekhem*. Both were offered to Sekhmet to please her and seek her favour in ritual. The latter was used to write her name and thus works as a direct symbol for Sekhmet herself. The inclusion of Hut-hor's bovine face on the hieroglyph strengthens this, especially when used as a symbol for invoking Sekhmet's more benevolent attributes.

The sun disc and the rearing uraeus cobra are obvious symbols of Sekhmet in her role as the Eye of Ra. They represent her apotropaic powers to both defend and attack. As well as being depicted as the sun disc and uraeus, the well-known symbol of the *Udjat* Eye could also function to represent the protective solar powers of Sekhmet as the Eye of Ra (fig. 5).

The colours red, orange, and yellow are ones closely associated with Sekhmet for obvious reasons. In ancient Egyptian magical practice, the colour red was associated with blood, as in menstrual and birth amulets; it was also associated with the sun and numerous chaotic forces (Raven, 2012, pp. 59-60). The title *nb.t-ins*, roughly pronounced *nebet-ines*, means 'Lady of the Red Linen', and was often a title associated with Sekhmet and Hut-hor (Eltoukhy, 2019, pp. 69, 76). This red linen might refer to blood-stained cloth, but also red fabric worn by her devotees and the Netjeret herself, representing her fiery attributes. One spell makes use of the red ribbons of Hut-hor to bind demons and prevent them from causing harm (Pinch, 2006, p. 81).

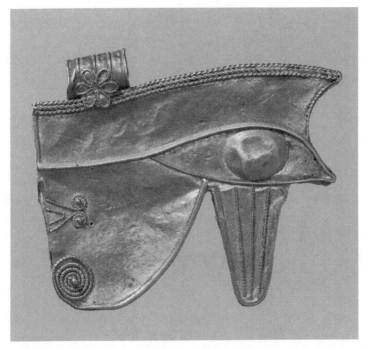

Figure 5. Udjat Eye amulet (Metropolitan Museum of Art 23.2.67)

Spells & Prayers

The following selection of spells and prayers demonstrate the mixed approach used by the ancient Egyptians towards Sekhmet, at times praying for her help and at others praying to be protected *from* her and her emissaries.

For Protection against Sekhmet

A spell entitled, 'The Book of the Last Day of the Year' commands the slaughterers of Sekhmet to be gone:

Hail to [you] gods there, murderers who stand in waiting upon Sakhmet, Who have come forth from the eye of Ra, messengers everywhere present in the districts, who bring slaughtering about, who create uproar, who hurry through the land, who shoot their arrows from their mouth, who see [from] afar! Be on your way, [be

distant] from me! Go on, you! I shall not go along with you! You shall have no power over me...
(Section from, *Papyrus Leiden,* 23A; no. 13, Borghouts, 1978, p. 12)

These words were to be recited over a piece of linen, adorned with images of several Netjeru and knotted twelve times, one knot for each month of the year. Offerings of bread, beer, and incense would be offered to these Netjeru and the knotted linen was to be worn around the neck at the New Year and/or the time of plague. Another spell invokes the Netjer, Khonsu to protect a young girl. It is written on a piece of linen which was rolled up and placed in a wearable wooden tube. Part of the spell says the following:

We shall protect her against Sekhmet and her son. We shall protect her against the collapse of walls and the impact of lightning. We shall protect her against leprosy, blindness and against the evil eye during her whole life...
(Raven, 2012, pp. 97-98)

Invoking Sekhmet's Protection

Alternatively, Sekhmet can be invoked, alongside other Netjeru to offer her protection, as in this spell protecting against the evil eye:

Sekhmet's arrow is in you, the heka of Thoth is in your body, Isis curses you, Nephthys punishes you, the lance of Horus is in your head... He blinds your eyes, all you people, all nobles, all common people, all the sun-folk and so on, who will cast an evil eye against [name] ... you will be slain like 'Apep, you will die and not live forever.
(No. 5, Borghouts, 1978, p. 2)

The Litany of Sekhmet, Invocation against the Seven Arrows of the Year

The *Litany of Sekhmet* appears on the walls of the temple of Edfu and was originally translated into French by Phillippe Germond. The litany lists Sekhmet's many epithets and in a rhythmic repetition it beseeches her to protect the king from harmful entities and diseases. It remains one of the best ancient texts in praise of Sekhmet there is, demonstrating her incredible power and complex nature. Provided below is a list of some of Sekhmet's epithets included in the litany, translated into English, from Germond's French translation of the original ancient Egyptian. They highlight the ways in which the ancient Egyptian priesthood viewed her at the time of the litany's creation. This is followed by the concluding stanzas, which are provided by Richard Reidy's 2010 English translation of Germond:

O Sekhmet, Eye of Ra, Great of Flame, Lady of protection who surrounds her creator!...

O Sekhmet, You who illuminate the Double Land with your flame and give the capacity of sight to all!...

O Sekhmet, Lady of Flame, Great of Flame, Great of Terror, in fear of whom the Double Land trembles!...

O Sekhmet, Uraeus upon the head of her master, who protects him with her flame!...

O Sekhmet, when you rise, the Light appears; when you go back, darkness comes!...

O Sekhmet, Lady of Slaughter the way you like, the one who turns her face toward the south, the north, the west, and the east, so that mankind is in fear!...

O Sekhmet, the one who spreads your terror upon everything, the one who has been asked for life by those who rest in your hand!...

O Sekhmet, more divine than the Netjeru, more glorious than the Ennead, Lady of Light, whose place is foremost upon the head of her Lord!...

O Sekhmet, the one who presides as the Power for capturing the Wanderers, Lady of Life of the Double Land, who can be the cause of death!...

O Sekhmet, the sight of whom reduces all things to ashes...

O Sekhmet, the one who shines, on account of whom one rejoices when it is ordered that her flame proceeds! When you shine, one rejoices because of you; [when] you are kind, the flame is appeased...

O Sekhmet, the one who fills the ways with blood, who slays to the limit of all she sees!...

O Sekhmet, the one who opens and one lives... Mistress of Life who awards according to her desire!...
(*The Litany of Sekhmet*; English translation based on that of Germond, 1981, 75-81).

The litany's concluding stanzas seek protection from the Seven Arrows. Sekhmet's epithets are spoken, followed by a repeated phrase and the arrow's number:

O Sekhmet, the one who presides over the country, Lady of Vegetation, Generous One, Sekhmet who protects the Double Land!
...

[repeat between epithet section and Arrow's number] *Come toward the King of Upper and Lower Egypt, the Lord of the Double Land, the Son of Ra, Lord of crowns, [name], the Living Image, the Living Falcon! Save him, protect him, (and) preserve him from the*

... First Arrow of the year!

O Sekhmet, the Curled One, Lady of Obscurity, Wadjet the Great!... Second Arrow of the year!

O Sekhmet, the one who moves in light, the one who terrifies the gods by her massacre!... Third Arrow of the year!

O Sekhmet, the one who guides mankind, Lady of the (Two) Shores, (and Lady) of humanity!... Fourth Arrow of the year!

O Sekhmet, Luminous One, the Great, preeminent in the Mansion of Fire, who terrorizes the Double Land by her fear!... Fifth Arrow of the year!

O Sekhmet, the one who loves Maat and who detests Evil, Lady of rekhyt... Sixth Arrow of the year!

O Sekhmet, Uraeus who opens the acacia, Sovereign (One), the Great!... Seventh Arrow of the year!
(English translation by Reidy, 2010 after Germond, 1981, 75-81).

Sa Sekhem Sahu
Robert Masters' popular book, *The Goddess Sekhmet: Psycho-Spiritual Exercises of the Fifth Way* (Masters, 2002) introduced many modern devotees of Sekhmet to a chant consisting of three ancient Egyptian words:
Sa,

Sekhem
Sahu!

Masters explains to readers that these words translate to 'The Breath of Life, The Sacred Might' and 'The Realized Human' (Masters, 2002, pp. 8-9, 73-74). Masters' took a degree of creative license in these translations. *Sa* usually means 'protection', *sekhem* indeed means 'power/might', and *sahu* refers to one of the spiritual bodies. This simple chant is widely used by devotees of Sekhmet today to call upon her presence and power and I have no doubt that she responds to well to it!

In Praise of Sekhmet
Hail to you, O Sekhmet, Mighty One, Lady of Flame! [shake sistrum]
Praise to you, O Sekhmet,
Untamed Lioness, Striking Serpent, and Avenging Eye! [shake sistrum]
Praise to you, O Sekhmet,
Dispenser of divine retribution, Sovereign of righteous rage! [shake sistrum]
Praise to you, O Sekhmet,
Mistress of Life, who shows mercy and affection towards her own... [shake sistrum]
Nebut Netjeret, (Golden Goddess)
Nebet Ankh Tawy, (Lady of the Life of the Two Lands)
Nebet Nebi, (Lady of Flame)
Iaret en Ra, (Uraeus of Ra) [shake sistrum]
May you turn your flaming gaze away from us, [shake sistrum]
May you rest your paws protectively upon us, [shake sistrum]
May you be jubilated, may you be appeased! [shake sistrum]
Dua Sekhmet! [shake sistrum]
(Author's own prayer, 2020)

A Contemporary Pagan Perspective

The spells and prayers offered here can be easily adapted for modern use. Given the continuing nature of disease in the world from localised outbreaks to pandemics, protective spells and prayers to ward off illness are still very relevant today, although, to be used in addition to responsible preventative measures. For many contemporary Pagans today, the New Year may not be celebrated at the same time as the ancient Egyptian calendar, around July or August. The New Year may also not be a time considered to be fraught with danger for many. Whilst remembering the ancient Egyptian context of these spells, and why this time of year was considered dangerous, Sekhmet's protective magic can be called upon at other times, as suggested in the previous chapters.

It is also a powerful thing to make use of the approximated pronunciation of ancient Egyptian words in such prayers, spells, or epithets. Egyptian priests during the second and third centuries CE believed that their language held power that translations into other languages could not replicate; nevertheless, today we simply have to make do with approximations and our fervent intentions.

Conclusion

Worshipping Sekhmet Today

Making an Altar/Shrine

For many contemporary Pagans, creating an altar or a shrine is an initial or primary way of physically expressing their intentions and spiritual devotion. If one is interested, or intent upon reviving Sekhmet's reverence in their spiritual path, creating an altar or shrine dedicated to her makes this intention clear and acts to invite her into one's life. An altar is a space where spiritual 'work' can take place, whereas a shrine is solely for the deity/ancestor/liminal entity's veneration. These are highly personalised spaces and are a physical expression of one's individual connection to Sekhmet. Through reading this book and others, as well as your own experiences, you will have some idea of what you feel is appropriate for an altar or shrine dedicated to Sekhmet. It will also depend upon whether you intend this space to be inspired by ancient Egyptian examples, or if you would prefer something more modern.

Ancient Egyptian altars were typically flat table-like surfaces whereupon offerings could be placed. Offering tables would be in the shape of the hieroglyph that spelt the word *hotep*, meaning 'offering' (and also 'peace'), and could be decorated with carvings of common offerings so that even when physical ones were not upon the table the Netjer was always in receipt of them (see British Museum, EA94). This reflected the belief that to depict something made it real. The cult icon would have been concealed within a rectangular box or niche covered by a door or cloth. The icon was considered to be alive and contain part of the essence of the Netjer; it was therefore offered the greatest respect and could only be looked upon by higher levels of the priesthood, with the exception of festival processions where the icon would be carried in public. The daily offering rituals would have involved uncovering the icon, placing offerings in front of it, and dressing it in linen (Teeter, 2011, pp. 47-48).

Modern Egyptian or Kemetic practitioners may choose to activate their icons through a ritual which opens the statue so that the Netjer can take residence there. Others may wish to use their icons as a representation only and therefore may not choose to keep them covered outside of ritual. Many modern Pagan altars are spaces where offerings can be made, usually using various vessels; they also commonly feature representations of deities as well as a number of decorative items. Therefore, the modern altar or shrine is different to ancient antecedents in this respect; however, within reason, they may not be completely unlike the altars and shrines of the common Egyptian people within their homes.

Some suggestions for a contemporary Sekhmet altar, would be to include an altar cloth coloured in various fiery shades, some candles, and a representation of Sekhmet, if possible. Representations can be through figurines imitating ancient examples, as well as 2D artwork and symbolic images such as lions, cobras, the *Udjat* Eye, or a sun disc. You could also write Sekhmet's name in hieroglyphs which would evoke her presence. Other potentially useful items would certainly be an offering vessel for liquid libations such as beer, as well as a musical percussion instrument imitating a sistrum rattle.

Recreating Rituals & Festivals

Chapter 6 outlined several rituals and festivals from antiquity that could be recreated today by Sekhmet's devotees. Common rituals would be those making offerings to Sekhmet with the intention of simply wanting to offer her devotion and thanks; other offerings may be made seeking her appeasement. Sekhmet's appeasement rituals can indeed be enacted during times of crisis or illness, seeking to calm her anger and baleful influences, to make her happy, and to encourage her favour.

Recreating or reviving ancient festivals and rituals are always conducted with a level of creative licence, although they exist upon a spectrum of historical authenticity and contemporary innovation. An example of a revived ritual in the 21st century is beautifully described by Sekhmet priestess Anne Key, who writes how she 'wanted to create a ceremony that honoured Sekhmet in all ways - with libations, incense, flowers, offerings, song, dance, fire' (Key, 2011a, p. 151). This annual ritual involved an evening procession of Sekhmet's icon upon a palanquin that was carried to her temple in the Nevada desert (Key, 2011a, p. 157). Ahead of the icon, participants cleared the way for Sekhmet using the four elements: two participants danced with fire poi, followed by celebrants sprinkling rose water, wafting *kyphi* incense, and ending with those spreading flowers upon Sekhmet's path. All participants wore red and the whole procession was followed by musicians. The procession culminated with a devotional ritual where Sekhmet's many epithets were recited (Key, 2011a, pp. 158-159). This is a good example of a modern ritual which takes inspiration from many historical features, albeit it is one intended for a group.

Contemporary Devotees

Many books and websites have been published by modern devotees of Sekhmet. It is striking how much this Netjeret of impressive antiquity and of ferocious reputation, from a time, and often place, far removed from our own, continues to inspire great devotion in people today. Something I really wanted to communicate through this introduction to Sekhmet is that she is a Netjeret who forces us to acknowledge the whole of nature, including those parts we may find disconcerting. There are many Pagan deities to worship/work with/revere who represent the abundant earth and offer us joy and comfort. Certainly, Sekhmet can provide these things, as well as fertility to some devotees. However, Sekhmet is also the scorching heat of the sun and fire. She is bringer of pestilence, which though devastating is perfectly within nature's laws. She is the aggressive protection sometimes needed by those in very real danger or suffering from a severe crisis in health. Sometimes nature isn't friendly. Sometimes nature isn't 'fair'. Sometimes people are cruel and killing adversaries with kindness isn't going to do the trick... Other Goddesses in world cultures likewise express these uncomfortable truths, whether it be Kali dancing with severed heads in her grasp, or the Morrigan whose screams can win battles through instilling death-wielding terror. From the ancient evidence at least, this is how many ancient Egyptians experienced Sekhmet and personally I absolutely love this side of her! For me, Sekhmet rears up as an uncompromising, ferocious, manifestation of female power. Through destruction she heals. Through destruction she protects. Through destruction she empowers. And through destruction she makes space for change and creation.

I believe that Sekhmet's ancient manifestations according to the Egyptian ancestors should be considered alongside the perspectives shared by their modern Egyptian descendants, and contemporary Pagan experiences of her. I therefore also completely support modern interpretations and experiences which highlight Sekhmet's healing, protective, and even maternal manifestations. As a contemporary polytheist I do not believe that deities remain static and frozen from their first appearances in human culture. I believe that Netjeru, like deities from other cultures, respond to their devotees and changing times. I believe that they travel with their devotees and are not limited to a single landscape - although they will always retain the memory and connection to their original land and culture. For this reason, I easily understand how many modern devotees may not focus on Sekhmet as the bringer of pestilence and instead experience her primarily as a healing Netjeret. I do believe that this is some of the ways that she is now presenting herself to many devotees, although her destructive side is nonetheless still acknowledged by most.

Sekhmet continues to inspire numinous experiences in pilgrims who visit her at Hut-hor's Karnak chapel and her various larger than life statues in museums across the world. Sekhmet clearly has something to say to us in the modern day. I hope that I have been able to provide an introduction to this wildly complex Netjeret, and that possibly Sekhmet's hot breath, rumbling growl, and protective paws have been able to reach you in some way through the words of this devotional work.

Dua Sekhmet, Eye of Ra, Lady of Flame!

Appendix

Key Egyptian Names and Words

Included here are the names of ancient Egyptian Netjeru who are more commonly known today in their Greek form. I encourage you to memorise the names that the Egyptians originally referred to them as, before their later international travel. I have also included a small selection of Middle Egyptian words that may be of interest. For ease of a suggested pronunciation I have written the Egyptian phonetically, though it should be noted that accurate pronunciation remains uncertain due to the lack of vowels in the written language.

NAMES		
	Egyptian	**Greek**
ꞽs.t	Aset	Isis (Goddess)
ḏḥwty	Djehuty	Thoth (God)
ḥwt-ḥr	Hut-hor	Hathor (Goddess)
ḥrw-wr	Heru-wer (also just Heru)	Horus the Elder (God)
ḥrw-sꞽ-ꞽs.t	Heru-sa-aset (also just Heru)	Horus son of Isis (God)
ḫꞽtjw	Khatiu	The Slaughterers
nb.t-ḥwt	Nebet-Hut	Nephthys
šmꞽjw	Shema-iu	The Wanderers
stḫ	Sutekh	Seth (God)
wsjr	Wesir	Osiris (God)

WORDS		
dwꞽ	*Dua*	Praise
m ḥtp	*Em Hotep*	In peace
ḥqꞽ	*Heka*	'Magic' (loose translation)
ḥm nṯr.t /	*Hem Netjeret*	Priest / Priestess of the

ḥm.t nṯr.t/	Hemet Netjeret	Goddess (more accurately
		'servant')
km.t	Kemet	Egypt
nb / nb.t	Neb / Nebet	Lord / Lady (can be
		used to address deities)
nṯr / nṯr.w /	Netjer / Netjeru / Netjeret	God / Gods (all genders)
nṯr.t / nṯr.wt	/ Netjerut	/ Goddess / Goddesses
sꜣ	Sa	Protection
sꜣ n / sꜣ.t n.t	Sa en / Sat net	Son of / Daughter of
sḥtp	Sehetep	Appeasement
snb.ty	Senebty	(May you) be healthy
šmꜣy.t	Shemayet	Chantress
šmsw	Shemsu	Follower
wꜥb / wꜥb.t	Wab / Wabet	Pure Priest /
		Pure Priestess

Bibliography

Primary Sources

Allen, James, P. (2007) Translation for MMA 13.182.3, 1. 6, Metropolitan Museum of Art online catalogue. Accessed 23 August 2020 <https://www.metmuseum.org/art/collection/search/544201>.

Allen, James, P. (2015) *The ancient Egyptian pyramid texts [translated] by James P. Allen*. Atlanta, SBL Press.

Borghouts, J. F. (1978) *Ancient Egyptian Magical Texts*. Leiden, Brill.

Breasted, James, Henry (1930) *The Edwin Smith Surgical Papyrus* (vol 1). Chicago, The University of Chicago Press.

British Museum online catalogue, items EA20791, EA20792, EA94. Accessed 2 May 2020 < https://research.britishmuseum.org/research/collection_online/search.aspx>.

Egypt Museum (2019) 'Golden Uraeus of Senusret II'. Accessed 4 October 2020 https://egypt-museum.com/post/187005755606/uraeus-of-senusret-ii#gsc.tab=0.

Faulkner, Raymond, O. (1937) 'The Bremner-Rhind Papyrus: III: D. The Book of Overthrowing 'Apep', *The Journal of Egyptian Archaeology*, vol. 23, no. 2, 166-185.

Faulkner, Raymond, O. (2007) *The Ancient Egyptian Coffin Texts*. Oxford, Aris et Phillips.

Herodotus, *The Histories. Book Two*. Trans. Godley, A. D (1920). Accessed 4 Oct 2020 <http://www.perseus.tufts.edu>

Kelly Simpson, William ed. (2003) *The Literature of Ancient Egypt: An Anthology of Stories, Instructions, Stelae, Autobiographies, and Poetry* (third edition). London, Yale University Press.

Lichtheim, M. (1973) *Ancient Egyptian Literature* (vol. 1). Berkeley, University of California Press.

Metropolitan Museum of Art, online catalogue, no. 550940. Accessed 3 October 2020 <https://www.metmuseum.org/art/

collection/search/550940>.

Scott, N. (1951) 'The Metternich Stela', *The Metropolitan Museum of Art Bulletin,* vol. 9, no. 8, 201-217

Walters Art Museum, online catalogue, no. 57.540. Accessed 25 August 2020. < https://art.thewalters.org/detail/39570/aegis-with-the-head-of-sakhmet/>.

Wente, Edward, F. (2003) 'The Book of the Heavenly Cow', in Kelly Simpson, William (ed.), *The Literature of Ancient Egypt: An Anthology of Stories, Instructions, Stelae, Autobiographies, and Poetry* (third edition). London, Yale University Press, pp. 289-298.

Secondary Sources

All Love website. 'About Patrick Zeigler'. Accessed 4 October 2020 <all-love.com/ourstory>.

Amgad, Joseph (2018) 'Divine Wrath in Ancient Egypt', Études et Travaux, vol. 31, 27-65.

Aziz, Sophia (2018) 'Sekhmet – Patron Goddess of Healers and Physicians', *Nile Magazine,* no. 11, 34-41.

Brewer, Douglas & Teeter, Emily (2007) *Egypt and the Egyptians.* Cambridge, Cambridge University Press.

Bryan, Betsy (1997) 'The statue program for the mortuary temple of Amenhotep III', in Quirke, Stephen (ed.) *The Temple in Ancient Egypt: New Discoveries and Recent Research.* London, British Museum Press, pp. 57-81.

Bryan, Betsy (2017) 'Sekhmet and Ritual Revelries in the Reign of Amenhotep III'. Paper given for the *Sekhmet Omnipresent* conference, The Mummification Museum in Luxor, Egypt, 23 March 2017.

Bryan, Betsy (2020) 'Altered State of Religion: Sekhmet and Ritual Revelries in the Reign of Amenhotep III'. Paper given for the ARCE online series on 30 September 2020.

Capel, Anne, K. & Markoe, Glenn. E. eds. (1997) *Mistress of the House, Mistress of Heaven: Women in Ancient Egypt.* New York,

Hudson Hills Press.

Capochichi, Sandro (2016) 'Towards a new interpretation of the myth of the Destruction of Mankind', *Cahiers Caribéens d'Egyptologie*, vo.l. 21, 47-60.

Darnell, John Coleman (1995) 'Hathor Returns to Medamûd', *Studien zur Altägyptischen Kultur*, vol. 22, 47-94.

Eltoukhy, M. (2019) 'The meaning of the world *ins* through ancient Egyptian hieroglyphic texts', *Egyptian Journal of Archaeological and Restoration Studies*, vol. 9, no. 1, 69–78.

Faulkner, Raymond, O. (1962) *A Concise Dictionary Middle Egyptian*. Oxford, Griffith Institute.

Gaber, Amr (2003) *'Aspects of the deification of some Old Kingdom kings', in Eyma, Aayko K. & Bennett, C. J. (eds.), A delta-man in Yebu. Occasional volume of the Egyptologists' electronic forum. Boca Raton, Universal Publishers*, 12-31.

Germond, Philippe (1981) *Sekhmet Et La Protection Du Monde*. Genève, Editions de Belles-Lettres.

Guilhou, Nadine (2010) 'Myth of the Heavenly Cow', *UCLA Encyclopedia of Egyptology*, vol. 1, no. 1, 1-7. Accessed 15 February 2020 <https://escholarship.org/uc/item/2vh551hn>.

Hendrickx, Stan (2013) 'Hunting and Social Complexity in Predynastic Egypt', in *Koninklijke Academie voor Overzeese Wetenschappen, Mededelingen der Zittingen*, vol. 57, 237-263.

Hendrickx, Stan, Huyge, Dirk & Wendrich, Willeke. (2010) 'Worship without Writing', in Wendrich, Willeke (ed.), *Egyptian Archaeology*. Malden, Blackwell Publishing, pp. 15-35.

Hornung, Erik (1996) *Conceptions of God in ancient Egypt: the one and the many. translated by John Baines*. New York, Cornell University Press.

Ikram, Salima (1995) *Choice Cuts: Meat Production in Ancient Egypt*. Leuven, Department Oosterse Studies.

Ikram, Salima (2003) *Death and Burial in Ancient Egypt*. London, Pearson Education.

Ikram, Salima (2012) 'Sacrifice, Pharaonic Egypt', *The Encyclopedia of Ancient History*. Doi <https://doi.org/10.1002/9781444338386. wbeah15004>.

Jensen, Victoria (2017) 'Predynastic precursors to the Festival of Drunkenness: beer, climate change, cow-goddesses, and the ideology of kingship', in Rosati, Gloria & Guidotti, Maria Cristina (eds.), *Proceedings of the XI International Congress of Egyptologists*. Oxford, Archaeopress Publishing, pp. 296-302.

Junker, Hermann (1911) *Der Auszug der Hathor-Tefnut aus Nubien*. Berlin, G. Reimer.

Key, Anne (2011a) *Desert Priestess: a memoir*. Las Vegas, Goddess Ink.

Key, Anne (2011b) 'Hymn to Sekhmet', in Kant, Candace & Key, Anne (eds.) *Heart of the Sun: An Anthology in Exaltation of Sekhmet*. Bloomington, iUniverse, pp. 85-88.

Lange, Eva (2016) 'The Lioness Goddess in the Old Kingdom Nile Delta: A Study in Local cult Topography', in Lippert, S.L., Schentuleit, M. & Stadler, M.A (eds.), *Sapientia Felicitas: Festschrift für Günter Vittmann zum 26*. Montpellier, Université Paul Valéry, pp. 301-323.

Lucarelli, Rita (2010) 'Demons (the malevolent and benevolent)', in Dieleman, Jacco, & Wendrich, Willeke (eds.), *UCLA Encyclopedia of Egyptology*. Los Angeles. Accessed 15 February 2020 < http://digital2.library.ucla.edu/viewItem. do?ark=21198/zz0025fks3>.

Lucid, Tamra & Pontiac, Ronnie (2018) 'Emergence of Sekhmet: Twelve Interviews', *Reality Sandwich* website. Posted 25 June 2018. Accessed 25 August 2020 < https://realitysandwich. com/323032/emergence-of-sekhmet-twelve-interviews/>.

Malek, Jakob (2003) 'The Old Kingdom', in Shaw, Ian (ed.), *The Oxford History of Ancient Egypt*. Oxford, Oxford University Press, pp. 83-107.

Masters, Robert (2002) *The Goddess Sekhmet: Psycho-Spiritual Exercises of the Fifth Way*. Ashland, White Cloud Press.

Pinch, Geraldine (2002) *Egyptian Mythology. A guide to the Gods, Goddesses and Traditions of Ancient Egypt*. Oxford, Oxford University Press.

Pinch, Geraldine (2006) *Magic in Ancient Egypt*. London, British Museum Press.

Poo, Mu-Chou (2009) *Wine and Wine Offering in the Religion of Ancient Egypt*. London, Routledge.

Raven, Maarten (2012) *Egyptian Magic. The Quest for Thoth's Book of Secrets*. Cairo, University of Cairo Press.

Preys, Rene (1999) 'Hathor, maîtresse des seize et la fête de la navigation à Dendera', *Revue d'égyptologie*, vol. 50, 259–268.

Reidy, Richard (2010) *Eternal Egypt. Ancient Rituals for the Modern World*. Bloomington, iUniverse.

Richter, Barbara, A. (2010) 'On the Heels of the Wandering Goddess: The Myth and the Festival at the Temples of the Wadi el-Hallel and Dendera', in Dolińska, M. & Beinlich, H (eds.), *Ägyptologische Tempeltagung: interconnections between temples*. Wiesbaden, Harrassowitz Verlag, pp. 155-186.

Ritner, Robert (2008) *The Mechanics of Ancient Egyptian Magical Practice*. Chicago, The Oriental Institute of the University of Chicago.

Roberts, Alison (1995) *Hathor Rising: The Serpent Power of Ancient Egypt*. Rottingdean, Northgate Publishers.

Sakr, Faiza Mahmoud (2005) 'New Foundation Deposits of Kom El-Hisn', *Studien Zur Altägyptischen Kultur*, vol. 33, 349–355.

Scully, Nicki (2017) *Sekhmet. Transformation in the Belly of the Goddess*. Toronto, Bear & Company.

Smoláriková, Květa (2002) *Abusir VII: Greek imports in Egypt: Graeco-Egyptian relations during the first millennium B.C.*. Prague, Czech Institute of Egyptology, Charles University.

Sourouzian, Hourig et al. (2016) 'Conservation Work at the Temple of Amenhotep III at Thebes, by the Colossi of Memnon and Amenhotep III Temple Conservation Project,' *CTT Conference*, 11 February 2016 in Luxor.

Stirling, Sheila, Z. (2011) 'Heart of the Lion', in Kant, Candace & Key, Anne (eds.) *Heart of the Sun: An Anthology in Exaltation of Sekhmet.* Bloomington, iUniverse, pp. 67-68.

Teeter, Emily (2011) *Religion and Ritual in Ancient Egypt.* Cambridge, Cambridge University Press.

Thiers, Christophe (2011) 'The Temple of Ptah at Karnak', *Egyptian Archaeology,* vol. 38, 20-24.

Toonen, W.H.J *et al.* (2019) 'Amenhotep III's Mansion of Millions of Years in Thebes (Luxor, Egypt): Submergence of high grounds by river floods and Nile sediments', *Journal of Archaeological Science, reports,* vol. 25, 195–205.

Vaughan, Genevieve (2011) 'Sekhmet, Guardian of the Paths between the Worlds', in Kant, Candace & Key, Anne (eds.) *Heart of the Sun: An Anthology in Exaltation of Sekhmet.* Bloomington, iUniverse, pp. 69-72.

Wesselman, Hank (2011) 'My Encounters with Sekhmet', in Kant, Candace & Key, Anne (eds.) *Heart of the Sun: An Anthology in Exaltation of Sekhmet.* Bloomington, iUniverse, pp. 104-111.

Wilkinson, Richard (2000) *The Complete Temples of Ancient Egypt.* London, Thames & Hudson.

Wilkinson, Richard (2003) *The Complete Gods and Goddesses of Ancient Egypt.* London, Thames & Hudson.

Wilkinson, Toby (2003) *Genesis of the Pharaohs: Dramatic new discoveries rewrite the origins of ancient Egypt.* London, Thames & Hudson.

Yoyotte, Jean (1980) 'Une monumentale litanie de granit. Les Sekhmet d'Aménophis III et la conjuration permanente de la Déesse dangereuse', *Bulletin de la société française d'égyptologie,* vol. 87-88, 46-75.

You may also like...

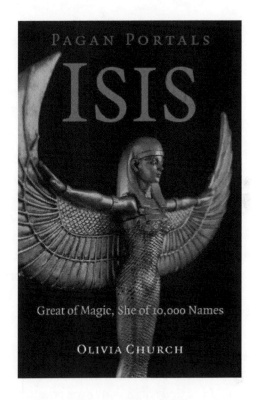

Pagan Portals – Isis
Great of Magic, She of 10,000 Names

978-1-78904-298-6 (Paperback)
978-1-78904-299-3 (e-book)

MOON
BOOKS

PAGANISM & SHAMANISM

What is Paganism? A religion, a spirituality, an alternative
belief system, nature worship? You can find support for all these
definitions (and many more) in dictionaries, encyclopaedias, and
text books of religion, but subscribe to any one and the truth will
evade you. Above all Paganism is a creative pursuit, an encounter
with reality, an exploration of meaning and an expression of the
soul. Druids, Heathens, Wiccans and others, all contribute their
insights and literary riches to the Pagan tradition. Moon Books
invites you to begin or to deepen your own encounter, right here,
right now.
If you have enjoyed this book, why not tell other readers by
posting a review on your preferred book site.

Recent bestsellers from Moon Books are:

Journey to the Dark Goddess
How to Return to Your Soul
Jane Meredith
Discover the powerful secrets of the Dark Goddess and transform your depression, grief and pain into healing and integration.
Paperback: 978-1-84694-677-6 ebook: 978-1-78099-223-5

Shamanic Reiki
Expanded Ways of Working with Universal Life Force Energy
Llyn Roberts, Robert Levy
Shamanism and Reiki are each powerful ways of healing; together, their power multiplies. *Shamanic Reiki* introduces techniques to help healers and Reiki practitioners tap ancient healing wisdom.
Paperback: 978-1-84694-037-8 ebook: 978-1-84694-650-9

Pagan Portals – The Awen Alone
Walking the Path of the Solitary Druid
Joanna van der Hoeven
An introductory guide for the solitary Druid, *The Awen Alone* will accompany you as you explore, and seek out your own place within the natural world.
Paperback: 978-1-78279-547-6 ebook: 978-1-78279-546-9

A Kitchen Witch's World of Magical Herbs & Plants
Rachel Patterson
A journey into the magical world of herbs and plants, filled with magical uses, folklore, history and practical magic. By popular writer, blogger and kitchen witch, Tansy Firedragon.
Paperback: 978-1-78279-621-3 ebook: 978-1-78279-620-6

Medicine for the Soul
The Complete Book of Shamanic Healing
Ross Heaven
All you will ever need to know about shamanic healing and how to
become your own shaman...
Paperback: 978-1-78099-419-2 ebook: 978-1-78099-420-8

Shaman Pathways – The Druid Shaman
Exploring the Celtic Otherworld
Danu Forest
A practical guide to Celtic shamanism with exercises and
techniques as well as traditional lore for exploring the Celtic
Otherworld.
Paperback: 978-1-78099-615-8 ebook: 978-1-78099-616-5

Traditional Witchcraft for the Woods and Forests
A Witch's Guide to the Woodland with Guided Meditations and
Pathworking
Mélusine Draco
A Witch's guide to walking alone in the woods, with guided
meditations and pathworking.
Paperback: 978-1-84694-803-9 ebook: 978-1-84694-804-6

Wild Earth, Wild Soul
A Manual for an Ecstatic Culture
Bill Pfeiffer
Imagine a nature-based culture so alive and so connected,
spreading like wildfire. This book is the first flame...
Paperback: 978-1-78099-187-0 ebook: 978-1-78099-188-7

Naming the Goddess
Trevor Greenfield
Naming the Goddess is written by over eighty adherents and
scholars of Goddess and Goddess Spirituality.
Paperback: 978-1-78279-476-9 ebook: 978-1-78279-475-2

Shapeshifting into Higher Consciousness
Heal and Transform Yourself and Our World with Ancient
Shamanic and Modern Methods
Llyn Roberts
Ancient and modern methods that you can use every day to
transform yourself and make a positive difference in the world.
Paperback: 978-1-84694-843-5 ebook: 978-1-84694-844-2

Readers of ebooks can buy or view any of these bestsellers by
clicking on the live link in the title. Most titles are published in
paperback and as an ebook. Paperbacks are available in traditional
bookshops. Both print and ebook formats are available online.

Find more titles and sign up to our readers' newsletter at
http://www.johnhuntpublishing.com/paganism
Follow us on Facebook at https://www.facebook.com/MoonBooks
and Twitter at https://twitter.com/MoonBooksJHP